Insurance
Perspectives

Insurance Perspectives

ROBERT J. GIBBONS, Ph.D., CPCU, CLU
Vice President
American Institute for CPCU

GEORGE E. REJDA, Ph.D., CLU
V.J. Skutt Professor of Insurance
University of Nebraska—Lincoln

MICHAEL W. ELLIOTT
Director of Curriculum
American Institute for CPCU

Coordinating Author
ERIC A. WIENING, CPCU, ARM, AU
Assistant Vice President
American Institute for CPCU

First Edition • 1992

AMERICAN INSTITUTE FOR
CHARTERED PROPERTY CASUALTY UNDERWRITERS
720 Providence Road, Malvern, Pennsylvania 19355-0716

Foreword

The American Institute for Chartered Property Casualty Underwriters and the Insurance Institute of America are independent, non-profit, educational organizations serving the needs of the property and liability insurance business. The Institutes develop a wide range of programs—curricula, study materials, and examinations—in response to the educational requirements of various elements of the business.

The American Institute confers the Chartered Property Casualty Underwriter (CPCU®) professional designation on those who meet the Institute's experience, ethics, and examination requirements.

The Insurance Institute of America offers associate designations and certificate programs in the following technical and managerial disciplines:

Accredited Adviser in Insurance (AAI®)
Associate in Claims (AIC)
Associate in Underwriting (AU)
Associate in Risk Management (ARM)
Associate in Loss Control Management (ALCM®)
Associate in Premium Auditing (APA®)
Associate in Management (AIM)
Associate in Research and Planning (ARP®)
Associate in Insurance Accounting and Finance (AIAF)
Associate in Automation Management (AAM®)
Associate in Marine Insurance Management (AMIM®)
Associate in Reinsurance (ARe)
Associate in Fidelity and Surety Bonding (AFSB)
Certificate in General Insurance
Certificate in Supervisory Management
Certificate in Introduction to Claims
Certificate in Introduction to Property and Liability Insurance

The Institutes began publishing textbooks in 1976 to help students meet the national examination standards. Since that time, we have produced more than seventy-five individual textbook volumes. Despite the vast differences in the subjects and purposes of these volumes, they all have much in common. First, each book is specifically designed to increase knowledge and develop skills that can improve job performance and help students achieve the educational objectives of the course for which it is assigned. Second, all of the manuscripts of our texts are widely reviewed prior to publication, by both insurance business practitioners and members of the academic community. In addition, all of our texts and course guides reflect the work of Institute staff members. These writing or editing duties are seen as an integral part of their professional responsibilities, and no one earns a royalty based on the sale of our texts. We have proceeded in this way to avoid even the appearance of any conflict of interests. Finally, the revisions of our texts often incorporate improvements suggested by students and course leaders.

We welcome criticisms of and suggestions for improving our publications. It is only with such constructive comments that we can hope to improve the quality of our study materials. Please direct any comments you may have on this text to the Curriculum Department of the Institutes.

Norman A. Baglini, Ph.D., CPCU, CLU
President and Chief Executive Officer

Preface

This text addresses some of the educational objectives of CPCU 1—Ethics, Insurance Perspectives, and Insurance Contract Analysis, one in a series of national examination courses leading to the Chartered Property Casualty Underwriter (CPCU) professional designation. CPCU national examinations are administered twice each year by the American Institute. The specific educational objectives evaluated through the national examination, as well as review questions and other study aids, appear in the CPCU 1 Course Guide, published by the American Institute and revised annually. Although designed to be used in conjunction with the CPCU 1 Course Guide and other assigned texts, this text also provides perspectives on insurance that may be of interest to other readers.

As a fundamental business institution, insurance has widespread ramifications. While each insurance transaction is a private contract, the results affect many people simultaneously. Those affected form opinions about the institution, and those opinions in turn influence the efficiency of insurance operations.

An educational program designed to prepare one for the practice of a profession should recognize the implications that profession has for society as a whole. While other parts of the CPCU program focus on essential technical aspects of property and liability insurance, this text therefore encourages readers to view insurance from a wider perspective. This perspective should enhance one's appreciation for the points of view of all those affected by insurance. To serve the needs of others, one must first ascertain and understand those needs.

Chapter 1 traces the evolution of insurance from early forms of risk distribution to the complex and highly regulated business practices of today. Its recurring theme is the ongoing adaptation of insurance practice to the changing needs and concerns of society. Current practice often has its roots in a past problem.

Chapter 2 places insurance in a risk management context. In this context one can evaluate insurance as a device for dealing with exposures to accidental loss in comparison with the alternatives. The chapter also surveys the diverse exposures typically covered by insurance.

Chapter 3 examines the rules under which society allows insurance to operate. The institution offers little security unless it is itself sound and viable. The problems inherent in promoting continuity in a competitive and dynamic economy are numerous, and those charged with such responsibility often differ from those they regulate in their concerns. This text does not attempt to prescribe solutions, only to clarify the issues.

The value of these perspectives appeared during the CPCU Curriculum Revision Project. The opinions of students, course leaders, agency and company executives, Institute staff members, and The Society of CPCU Curriculum Liaison Committee revealed the need for a broader understanding of insurance and its interaction with society. We are indebted to all who contributed their time and ideas to this project.

We are especially grateful to G. William Glendenning, Ph.D., CPCU, for his final review of the manuscripts for Chapters 2 and 3. Many improvements resulted from his work on the semi-final manuscript. We are also grateful to the following reviewers of portions of this text in earlier drafts, who offered many suggestions for improvement. These reviewers include Michael L. Averill, CPCU, Vice President, The Home Group; Paul A. Baiocchi, CPCU, AMIM, ARP, ARM, President, American Association of Insurance Services; James E. Brennan, CPCU, CLU, CIC, Professor/Consultant, University of Connecticut; Arthur L. Flitner, CPCU, ARM, Director of Curriculum, American Institute for CPCU; Karen L. Hamilton, Ph.D., Assistant Director of Curriculum, American Institute for CPCU; Sheila Mulrennan, President, The Insurance Archeological Group; Harry F. Perlet, Jr., J.D., CPCU, CLU, FLMI, attorney at law; John A. Reiner, CPCU, Assistant Vice President-Product Development, Crum & Forster; Dennis J. Ryan, CPCU, AU, Corporate Training Coordinator, PHICO; Carol W. Smith, Archivist, Green Tree Group; Jerome Trupin, CPCU, CLU, Trupin Insurance Services; and Bernard L. Webb, CPCU, FCAS, MAAA, Professor Emeritus of Actuarial Science, Risk Management, and Insurance, Georgia State University. In spite of the vigilance of this group of individuals, some inaccuracies and personal biases might remain in the text. The authors accept responsibility for any such flaws and urge readers who discover them to inform the Curriculum Department of the Institute.

Robert J. Gibbons
George E. Rejda
Michael W. Elliott

Contributing Author

The American Institute for Chartered Property Casualty Underwriters acknowledges with deep appreciation the help of the following contributing author:

Kim B. Staking, Ph.D.
Financial Economist
Inter-American Development Bank

Table of Contents

CHAPTER 1

Evolution of Insurance

Insurance today may be viewed as a complex, regulated business network providing a variety of products and services that help individuals, families, businesses, and other organizations to manage their risks. However, insurance was not always complicated. Basic tools of insurance have been used for many centuries. Over time, simple risk distribution techniques gradually evolved into their current complex form.

The evolution of insurance paralleled the evolution of legal systems, accounting systems, and other commercial systems. Merchants and other business people learned to use insurance techniques to mitigate the risks inherent in their business, just as they learned to use contracts to formalize their agreements and accounting methods to manage their finances. In the past, people were simply willing to accept many of the risks they faced or to rely on families, friends, religious communities, or other informal mechanisms for assistance in time of need. The growing complexity of modern life has led them increasingly to seek greater security against risks, through formal insurance mechanisms.

Insurance techniques appeared in the civilizations of Asia and the Islamic Middle East, as well as in medieval Europe. The expansion of the European economy eventually spread its institutions and business techniques to North America and the rest of the world. In the United States, the continual interplay between business entrepreneurs and government authority created a multifaceted regulatory environment that attempts to balance innovation and equity. The complex practices of the modern insurance world often exist simply because they seemed necessary at a particular time. Thus one good way to understand the insurance business of the present is to study its past.

EARLY DISTRIBUTION OF RISK

The idea of spreading or transferring risk appeared in many contexts in early times. Some examples arose in connection with shipping,

1

agriculture, shelter, and burials:

- *Shipping.* When property is being moved from one place to another, the chance of loss increases. Consider, for example, the problem facing Chinese merchants shipping their goods on the Yangtze River. Since some stretches of the Yangtze were treacherous, it was not unusual for the river to destroy both a boat and its cargo, a disaster for the merchant who owned that cargo. Therefore, each merchant spread his cargo among several boats instead of putting it all in one boat. This way each boat carried the cargo of several merchants. If the river destroyed a boat before it reached its destination, several merchants suffered a minor loss instead of one merchant suffering a disastrous loss. By dividing their shipments among several boats, these merchants were able to spread the risk of loss.

- *Agriculture.* Farming is a good example of a risky activity. Spring planting usually leads to fall harvests, but weather and pests can intervene. Patterns of land holdings in the Middle Ages show that farmers often held scattered fields in separate strips here and there rather than a single compact plot. This scattering would be considered an inefficient arrangement today, requiring each farmer to travel greater distances to tend the several fields. It probably reduced agricultural production by 10 or 15 percent. However, it also reduced the annual variation in the total crop yields of each farmer. In the Middle Ages it was an effective way to spread the risk of disastrous shortfalls in the harvest. When other forms of insurance against bad harvests, such as storage of grain, became more feasible, the pattern of scattered fields died out.[1]

- *Barn Raisings.* Another example of risk distribution appears in close-knit communities, such as the Amish communities of rural Pennsylvania and Ohio. The tradition of these communities provides that, when disaster strikes a family within the community and destroys its house or its barn, the entire community helps to rebuild the damaged structure. The same tradition of community assistance helps a newly-married couple build their first home. The resources of the community are pooled and applied where there is a need.

  Similar direct exchanges of risk are found in other rural areas with (often informal) networks that help rebuild properties lost to fire or other adverse circumstances.

- *Burial Societies.* A form of life insurance was applied in early burial societies, which were developed to cover the burial costs of group members. While this cost might have been large if it fell on the families of the individual members who died, it was considered a minor cost for each of the hundred or so members who constituted the society.

These examples of mutual assistance demonstrate techniques used to distribute risk over a larger community, in some cases even before the development of money and written contracts. These methods of risk distribution were undertaken without remuneration to those who did the work, other than the implicit promise that similar support would be provided to each member of the community when needed. Some members of the community were repaying past community actions, others would collect in the future, and some might never have the need for similar services. Nevertheless, all were willing to share in these primitive insurance relationships.

The concept of pooling and transferring risk was apparent in these and many other arrangements present in primitive society. The concept was well understood and widely practiced. Only in modern times, however, has insurance developed a scientific basis to measure the extent of the risks transferred.[2]

MARINE INSURANCE AND TRADE

A trade is a voluntary exchange of one thing for another. Because it allows them to rearrange their holdings, both parties can benefit from the exchange. If one has too much food and another too much cloth, both can improve their positions by making a trade. The costs of arranging the trade and the uncertainty surrounding its outcome, however, often hinder such exchanges.

Long-Distance Trade

Difficulties are especially apparent in long-distance trade. Trade over long distances can present attractive opportunities for profit, but also significant challenges.

Basis of Trade. Price differentials between locations create an incentive for long distance trade. If a commodity commands a higher price elsewhere, and the difference more than covers the cost of getting it there, a profit opportunity exists for the merchant willing to ship his goods to the remote market.

High Values. Trade-related profit opportunities appear most readily in the case of high-value goods. Items that are generally scarce, or goods that are unique to certain regions of the world but are also coveted elsewhere, may command widely differing prices in different locations. If these items are also small and easily transported, they provide an ideal basis of trade. The Asiatic spices used by Europeans to preserve their meats and fish are a good example. To obtain these spices, Europeans had to trade woolen cloth or other goods desired in Asia. The merchants who bought from one and sold to the other could make a profit if everything went according to plan.

Inventories. Even low-value commodities are traded over long distances if there are surpluses in one area and shortages in another. Merchants often stockpile such goods because they know their value to others. Thus a ready market exists, and some people buy or sell simply because the price is right. The sheer volume of trade in basic commodities is itself an inducement to further trade.

Payment Problems. Any exchange involves a trade of one thing for another. Some trades can be arranged on the spot, with each party making immediate delivery. Long distance trade, however, introduced some significant payment problems. In essence, these problems relate to distance, time, and uncertainty.

Distance. By definition, payment for a long-distance trade cannot be completed on the spot but must be executed through some sort of intermediary. During the Middle Ages the natural intermediary was the deposit banker. The word "bank" derives from the same root as the word "bench"—the original banker sat behind a bench in the marketplace and exchanged currencies. A natural outgrowth of this business was deposit banking. Since the banker had to keep his own money in a secure place overnight, he offered to safeguard the money of others in the same way. One could deposit funds with the banker, obtaining a receipt for the deposit, and redeem the funds later when needed.

The banker, therefore, had to keep accounts for his depositors. If the banker had connections in another city, perhaps a relative or business partner, funds could be received at one location and dispensed at another by making the appropriate entries in the accounts. This procedure solved the problem of making payment at a distant location.

Time. A remote transaction differed from a spot transaction in the time required to complete the payment. While the bankers solved the problem of transferring payments over long distances, the procedure took time. Funds to be received at some time in the future had less value to a merchant than funds received immediately. The modern practice of adding interest charges was generally condemned as usury in the Middle Ages, but the economic reality of money's time value remained.

Bankers solved this problem through the use of a "bill of exchange." The bill of exchange was the payment order issued by a banker in one location directing a banker in another location to dispense funds from a particular account. Often, different currencies prevailed in the two

locations, and the bill of exchange provided for the funds to be disbursed
in the local currency. An explicit amount in one currency (perhaps English pounds) was received by the banker who issued the bill of exchange,
and an explicit amount in another currency (perhaps Florentine florins)
was disbursed in another location. Without any explicit mention of interest, the bill of exchange often included a differential between the amount
received and the amount disbursed that reflected the time value of the
money.

Uncertainty. A third problem with long distance trade was the
uncertainty surrounding the execution of the transaction. Goods shipped
to a remote location might not arrive because of storms, thieves, or
unpredictable events of many kinds. The solution to this problem was a
contract of insurance that provided a source of recovery in case the
goods were lost. The first people to write such insurance contracts often
were the merchants and bankers already familiar with the other aspects
of medieval commerce.

Commercial Contracts

Europeans learned to put their agreements in writing in case
differing interpretations arose later. Many of the commercial arrangements that evolved during the Middle Ages involved attempts to share
risk. For the merchants engaged in long distance trade, these arrangements were a virtual necessity. The fact that goods could easily be
transported also meant that they could easily be lost or stolen. Their
opportunities for profit also involved great risk.

Partnerships. The simplest way to spread risk was to share it.
The earliest commercial contracts created various types of partnerships.
When one party had goods to transport and another had a ship available,
they could form a joint venture to take the goods to a distant port, sell
them, and split the profit. If the ship carrying the goods did not arrive,
they then shared in the loss. Partnerships also served as credit arrangements when one partner supplied the funds and the other partner managed the venture. More complicated contracts of this sort evolved that
shared the elements of business ventures—initial capital, labor, risk,
and profit—in various ways.

Marine Loans. A more specialized type of contract was a marine
loan. As used by Phoenicians, Greeks, Romans, and medieval Europeans,
a marine loan provided capital for a voyage with the ship or its cargo as
the collateral for the loan. If the ship or cargo was lost through no fault
of the borrower, the debt was canceled. If the ship and cargo arrived
safely, the cargo was sold and the loan repaid with an additional amount
to cover both interest on the loan and a risk premium (an extra charge

reflecting the risk of loss). Such marine loans were called "bottomry loans" when the ship served as collateral and "respondentia loans" when the cargo was the collateral.[3]

Marine Insurance.   Eventually these elements were separated, and it became possible to transfer the risk of loss, in return for a premium, separately from the financing and outfitting of the voyage. Even as separate transactions, however, these business arrangements were so related that often they were completed at nearly the same time and place.

Marine Insurance Markets

While marine insurance contracts developed to meet the needs of medieval commerce, they would have been useless unless parties could be found to take up both sides of such contracts. It was easier to arrange insurance in a city where there was already some experience with it. Thus certain locations emerged where interested parties tended to concentrate. These cities acquired reputations as active markets for insurance. Over the centuries, as political and technological circumstances influenced economic life, the leading European centers of the insurance market shifted from the Italian cities to the great trading centers of northwest Europe: Antwerp, then Amsterdam, and finally London.

Italian Cities.   The earliest surviving insurance contracts were written in Genoa, Pisa, Florence, and Venice. Merchants of these cities dominated the long distance trade of the fourteenth century.

Although medieval merchants combined the business of insurance with other trading activity, insurance was not always profitable for them. Only those with sufficient wealth could afford to bear the risk. Those who wrote insurance expecting no losses learned to regret their mistake. One example was an Italian merchant named Guiglielmo Barberi, who insured a bale of cloth and a barrel of furs on board a vessel sailing from Bruges to Barcelona. When pirates attacked and plundered the ship before it reached its destination, Barberi wrote to his correspondents in Spain begging them to search for the missing goods because he could not afford to pay for the loss. Having learned his lesson the hard way, he added: "for even though I were to live a thousand years, never again would I underwrite insurance."[4]

Antwerp.   By 1500 the northwestern corner of Europe had become the strategic center of much of the long distance trade. Antwerp, in present day Belgium, emerged as the commercial center of Europe. Everything, including insurance, could be purchased there, and the city was full of merchants, lawyers, clerks, and other experts in all the business techniques of the day. Transactions were recorded, and prices were established for nearly everything, including various types of risks. Even more important, Antwerp also provided a chamber for the resolution of insurance contract disputes.

Amsterdam. By the seventeenth century, Antwerp's northern neighbor, Amsterdam, took its place as the trading center of Europe. Commercial enterprise became the lifeblood of the Dutch Republic, and its citizens found ever more efficient ways to conduct business. They used partnerships to spread risk of loss of ships into sixty-four parts.[5] They traded with literally all parts of the world, and Amsterdam became a great storehouse of goods waiting to be sold.

The city quickly established the institutions to facilitate this far-flung commerce. In 1598, Amsterdam established a chamber of insurance. The Amsterdam Exchange Bank, founded in 1609, performed banking services and transfers free of charge, and the city made itself liable for deposits in the bank.[6] The Amsterdam Bourse, erected in 1609, became the world's first stock market. It also served as the center of a flourishing market in marine insurance. As a convenience for merchants shipping their goods abroad, the Bourse had stalls located next to one another to serve insurance, credit, and shipping needs.[7]

London. England also emerged from the Middle Ages as a trading nation. Its trade with the European continent centered around the southeastern ports and the capital, London. The Italian forms of marine insurance contracts were used there from at least the fifteenth century. London merchants acted as underwriters in these insurance contracts, which were negotiated by general commodity brokers. Notaries drafted and delivered the policies, and they kept registers of all the policies written. A Chamber of Assurances was established in 1576, and until 1690 all policies written had to be registered in its office in the Royal Exchange.

An Act of Parliament of 1601 recognized the legal status of marine insurance contracts. According to this act, "by means of which policies of assurance it cometh to pass on the perishing of any ship there followeth not the undoing of any man but the loss lighteth rather easily upon many than heavily upon few." Thus the benefits of insurance justified legal sanction, and the government stood ready to enforce insurance contracts and resolve disputes.

By the end of the seventeenth century, individuals interested in outfitting voyages or investing in such ventures often gathered at Edward Lloyd's Coffee House on Lombard Street near the Royal Exchange. It became customary for those gathered there to arrange mutual contracts of insurance against the perils of the sea to which their ventures were exposed. When notices of prospective voyages appeared describing the ship, its cargo, master, crew, and destination, individuals *wrote* their names and the amount of liability they would assume *under* the description of those voyages they were willing to back. For this reason, those insuring a voyage became known as *underwriters*. Each underwriter pledged his personal assets to cover the specified share of any insured loss. In return, the underwriter collected a premium. When the total amount exposed to loss was subscribed, the contract was complete.

For a brief time, Lloyd published a newspaper, *Lloyd's News*, that emphasized shipping news. Because of its connection with shipping interests, the coffee house served as the center of the marine insurance market and became known as Lloyd's of London in the early 1700s. Although it was only an association of individual underwriters, rather than an insurance company, Lloyd's offered all the necessary facilities for an effective market in marine insurance.

The London Stock Exchange developed around the same time as new enterprises were organized to take advantage of the opportunities present in the expanding British Empire. *Joint-stock companies* such as the East India Company, the South Sea Company, and the Royal African Company raised capital by selling stock in the enterprise to investors who shared in the profits, but risked no more than the amount of their respective investments. Speculative investments in these early joint-stock companies led to a crash known as the South Sea Bubble in 1720.

Parliament responded by passing the Bubble Act, which restricted limited liability to only those companies chartered by the Crown. Only two companies were authorized to sell marine insurance, the London Assurance and the Royal Exchange. This restriction worked to the advantage of the Lloyd's market by limiting its competition to only these two companies, and they devoted much of their attention to fire and life insurance. Thus during the eighteenth century Lloyd's developed into the major market for marine insurance in the British Isles and rivaled Amsterdam's facilities for marine insurance.

A standard marine policy was adopted in 1779. In 1795 an act of Parliament made this "Lloyd's Policy" the standard policy for all marine insurers. The Society of Lloyds was incorporated by an Act of Parliament in 1871 and has continued to operate under its own formal rules and informal customs.

LIFE INSURANCE

The evolution of life insurance added significantly to the development of certain insurance principles. While burial societies and other forms of life insurance can be found much earlier, during the seventeenth century life insurance became a widely practiced technique for providing financial security.

Statistical Basis for Life Insurance

One essential element in the evolution of life insurance was the development of statistics. The appropriate price for a life insurance contract depended on the probability of the insured's death. In the seventeenth century, mathematicians began to construct mortality tables by observing the number of deaths each year in a certain city.

Mortality Tables. The study of vital statistics started when an English shopkeeper named John Graunt analyzed the parish records of births and deaths in London from 1604 to 1661. His compilations of the number of deaths from various causes and other conclusions were published in a book called *Natural and Political Observations Made Upon the Bills of Mortality* in 1662. While Graunt's book contained some wise inferences drawn from his data, its main contemporary influence was to demonstrate the value of gathering data.[8] The book went through several editions and spread throughout England, France, and Germany the interest in gathering statistics.

The scientist Edmund Halley (the discoverer of Halley's comet) expanded on Graunt's work by studying the records of the city of Breslau in Germany. Because these records were more complete than any in England, they enabled Halley to analyze the frequency of death of persons at various ages. The result was a mortality table, such as the kind now used as a basis for life insurance rates.

Another mortality table was the work of Jan deWitt, the Amsterdam merchant who guided the political affairs of the Netherlands during the middle years of the seventeenth century. By linking his table of lives to the government's sale of bonds, deWitt was able to strengthen the finances of the state. The state needed to raise funds to support its military expenditures. By consistently honoring its debts, the government of the Netherlands had long had more success than other governments in raising funds. Thus a free market for government bonds emerged in which citizens with funds to invest were willing to buy government bonds that paid interest. Both buyers and sellers met their needs in this market for government bonds. The annuities offered by deWitt met the additional need some citizens had for financial security in future years. Since the government paid out funds only as long as the beneficiary of the annuity continued to live, it raised funds even more cheaply this way. The exact price of the annuity depended on the age of the insured, thus reflecting the probability of death deWitt calculated from his mortality table.[9]

These mortality tables were the raw material for the early development of the field of statistics. The essential precondition for the analysis of a collection of data was that the data represented measurements made under conditions that could be considered identical. Whereas most human events can be associated with a variety of variables and thus explained in many different ways, life or death, as well as age, was definite and objective.

Law of Large Numbers. A fundamental problem for statisticians is the measurement of uncertainty. During the seventeenth century Pascal and many other mathematicians studied games of chance and developed the rules of combinations, permutations, and other aspects of probability. As the work of Descartes, Newton, and Leibnitz led to the development of calculus, mathematics became increasingly formal. That is, mathematicians tried not only to infer previously unrecognized relationships (rules), but also to develop logical proofs to demonstrate these relationships convincingly.

The great Swiss mathematician, Jacob Bernoulli, developed the first proof (published posthumously in 1713) of a rule that is the basis for the modern practice of insurance. Bernoulli considered this rule, which has come to be known as the law of large numbers, to be well known already. "For even the most stupid of men," he wrote, "by some instinct of nature, by himself and without any instruction (which is a remarkable thing), is convinced that the more observations have been made, the less danger there is of wandering from one's goal."[10] Bernoulli's formal proof of the law of large numbers not only demonstrated that uncertainty can be reduced by increasing the number of observations but also showed how that principle could be quantified.

Growth of a Wage Economy

A second essential element in this evolution was the growing use of money in the economy and the possibility for converting goods and services into instruments that could be readily bought and sold. As people tended to earn their living in money wages rather than in the goods they produced, wage replacement to protect widows and surviving children became increasingly important. Thus life insurance became a means of saving for an uncertain future.

In Britain the life insurance business grew dramatically in the first half of the nineteenth century, a time associated with the virtues of thrift and frugality espoused in the Victorian era. The number of life insurance offices increased from six to about 150, and the amount of life insurance in force increased from about ten million to nearly 150 million pounds during this time.

Credit Enhancement

A third significant factor in the growth of life insurance was its use mitigating the risks inherent in other business transactions. Often, an "other-interest policy" was sold on the life of a businessman whose death would otherwise have a disastrous effect on the other party to a business arrangement.[11]

FIRE INSURANCE

As the population of cities grew, so did the danger of fire. The scientific methods used in life insurance encouraged similar attempts at fire insurance. During the seventeenth century several German cities developed fire insurance techniques, and these techniques were soon imitated elsewhere.

The Great Fire of London in 1666 demonstrated the destructive potential of fire in an urban environment. London had no organized municipal fire protection. As houses were rebuilt following the fire, the owners worried about a possible recurrence. One entrepreneur named Nicholas Barbon conceived a speculative business operation involving residential construction and sales. Each sale included an agreement to repair or rebuild any house damaged or demolished by fire. The scheme met such widespread acceptance that Barbon expanded his business to include a separate "Insurance Office for Houses," established in 1680 near the Royal Exchange in London. This fire office, like others that followed, maintained a group of firefighters ready to combat fire and prevent its spread in any property insured by the office. Barbon's fire office placed on each insured dwelling a distinctive metal insignia, or "fire mark," a practice widely imitated in subsequent years.

By 1684, another fire insurer was organized when participants in the Friendly Society agreed to share in fire losses as they occurred. Still another mutual fire office was known as the Hand-in-Hand, established in 1696. Then in 1710 Charles Povey founded the Sun Fire Office, the oldest insurance company still in existence in Britain and now part of the Sun Alliance. Although started as a partnership, Sun converted to a joint-stock company in 1726. The Sun Fire Office expanded rapidly and easily gained the advantage over the mutual fire offices.

These companies concentrated on the insurance of private houses and therefore wrote most of their business in the city of London. The Sun wrote some business outside of London during the early eighteenth century, even as far as Wales and Scotland, but it found that insurance was not well understood outside of London. To expand its business into the country, Sun appointed agents to represent it. Although it appointed only thirty agents in its first twenty years, by 1786 Sun conducted its business through 123 local agencies. The busiest agencies were in major country towns, such as Exeter, Canterbury, Winchester, York, and Edinburgh.

In the latter half of the eighteenth century, fire insurance expanded not only geographically, but also in the types of structures it covered. Houses and shops continued to account for the greatest number of policies; and breweries, cotton mills, warehouses, printing works, flour mills, and sugar refineries provided additional business for the fire offices. When buildings were under construction or inventories expanded, it was not unusual for new policies to be issued every few weeks to provide for the increasing value of the property and perhaps to monitor increased hazards.

INSURANCE IN THE UNITED STATES

Insurance in the United States evolved from the familiar practices of the British Empire into an enormous, but distinctive market. Marine, fire, and life insurance were easily transplanted from England to colonial America, but as the new country grew, new forms and conditions of insurance emerged as well. The earliest American insurers were individual underwriters or policyholder-owned mutual insurance companies. Later, it became possible to raise capital from stockholders and from stock insurance companies.

Marine Insurance in Colonial America

The seaport cities of colonial America developed the same need for marine insurance that European seaports already had. Two significant obstacles, however, arose because they were British colonies. First was the shortage of capital because of their small size. The second was their inability to form joint-stock companies, which would have enabled them to gather capital more efficiently. This limitation was part of the price of belonging to the British Empire, since the Parliamentary restriction of new corporations to write insurance applied in the colonies as well.

As markets in Amsterdam and London perfected the technique of marine insurance during the eighteenth century, it became a routine element of maritime commerce. Colonial merchants tended to obtain their insurance in London, but sometimes only after a long delay because of the distance. Gradually agents in the major colonial ports—Boston, New York, Philadelphia, Baltimore, and Charleston—accepted applications for marine insurance and offered them to local underwriters. This practice resembled the operation of Lloyd's of London. Individual underwriters in the colonial ports, however, could not supply sufficient capital to meet the demand.

For example, Thomas Willing, the most prominent underwriter in colonial Philadelphia, was also among the city's wealthiest merchants.

He owned three ships, skillfully managed a vigorous trade with Europe and the Caribbean, and inherited a substantial fortune from his merchant father, who had also been twice mayor of the city. Even so, his total assets in 1754 amounted to only 10,000 pounds.[12]

The Act of Parliament of 1719 that established the Royal Exchange and the London Assurance expressly prohibited the formation of other stock insurance companies in the British Empire. In fact no joint stock corporations whatever were permitted in the American colonies. This limitation inhibited the accumulation of capital and slowed the development of the insurance business in the colonies.

The Declaration of Independence removed these constraints of British law. By October 1776 two marine insurance companies were formed in Charleston, South Carolina. Even the fragmentary records of these companies suggest their substantial size relative to individual underwriters. The Charleston Insurance Company contributed 3,000 pounds to assist the South Carolina Navy in recruiting seamen and invested 109,325 pounds in South Carolina bonds. The South Carolina Insurance Company, which had stated capital of 100,000 pounds, invested 160,725 pounds in South Carolina bonds. When the British army recaptured Charleston on May 12, 1780, these two companies became illegal under British law, which was restored there until the British government recognized American independence in 1783.[13]

Once the United States became an independent country and the Constitution provided it a settled form of government, joint stock companies, organized with limited liability for their investors, raised more capital for insurance operations. In 1792 the Insurance Company of North America was established in Philadelphia. It was incorporated under a Pennsylvania charter with $600,000 capital in 1794. It invested its excess funds in new enterprises of the country, and it established agents in foreign ports for settling claims. The establishment of the Insurance Company of North American freed American shipowners from their reliance on London underwriters. Its success prompted the formation of more marine insurers in other port cities.

The Napoleonic Wars provided an additional incentive. The owner of an American ship seized by the British could not recover its loss from Lloyd's or any other insurer in England. However, the disruption of American shipping resulting from Thomas Jefferson's embargo in 1807 and the War of 1812 caused many marine insurers to suspend operations or emphasize other lines of insurance.

Another marine insurer, the Atlantic, was organized in 1824 but suspended underwriting during a period of rate-cutting in 1826. It resumed business in 1829 and reorganized in 1842 as a mutual company. Atlantic Mutual, like other marine insurers, prospered during the great age of the American clipper ships, but it was one of the few New York companies to survive the difficult period following the Civil War. In that period, British steam-propelled metal ships carried an ever increasing proportion of American exports, and in this era of free trade British insurers captured most of the marine insurance market. Of the thirteen domestic marine insurers listed in the first report of the New York Insurance Department in 1864, only Atlantic Mutual has survived.

British domination of hull insurance was almost complete, since most ships were British and the British market dictated the hull insurance contract forms. American insurers continued to write a significant amount of cargo insurance. The revival of the American merchant marine early in the twentieth century improved conditions for American marine insurers. The formation of the American Institute of Marine Underwriters in 1920 helped the American companies regain some hull insurance business on a syndicated basis.

Fire Insurance

By the end of the eighteenth century, fire insurance and life insurance as well as marine insurance had become established lines of business in the United States. Fire insurance companies began in several colonial cities.

Charleston. The earliest known fire insurer in America was the Friendly Society for the Mutual Insuring of Houses against Fire, organized in Charleston, South Carolina, in 1735. Each member of the society insuring a house paid a premium of one percent of the value into a fund that was invested until needed. Each member also agreed to pay the proportionate share of the damage resulting from a fire to any other member's house, as determined by the directors of the society. On November 18, 1740, however, a single fire destroyed three hundred houses, over half the town of Charleston. After three months, the directors gave notice that they would bring suit against the members who still had not paid their obligations, but few of them were able to pay the sums required after a disaster of that magnitude. The company folded as a result.[14]

Philadelphia. Philadelphia residents were more fortunate. William Penn had planned the city as a grid of orderly blocks, in part to minimize, by separating buildings, the danger of fire. By the middle of the eighteenth century, Philadelphia had grown to become one of the largest cities of the British Empire. Its thriving trade led to a great increase in population and the construction of many buildings in the city. The city's most famous citizen, Benjamin Franklin, was well aware of the danger of fire in the city. His often-cited *Poor Richard's Almanac* noted regarding September 2 that on that date in 1666 "began the fire of London, which reduc'd to ashes 13,200 houses and 89 churches: Near ten times as much building as Philadelphia."[15]

Franklin's attempts to mitigate the danger of fire paralleled his other interests that promoted "the good of mankind": libraries, schools, hospitals, street lighting, and many similar civic improvements. He advocated the adoption of such new practices as smallpox inoculations and lightning rods because they made life healthier and more secure.[16]

Fire was a particular concern for Franklin. His famous saying, "An ounce of prevention is worth a pound of cure," first appeared in a newspaper editorial "On the Protection of Towns from Fire."[17] Insurance underwriters and risk managers still strive to apply the same principle. Franklin worked to improve the night watch so that fires might be discovered more quickly. Axes, Franklin believed, were useful in fighting fires. Even his experiments with electricity were motivated by his desire to understand lightning and alleviate it as a cause of fire.

By 1736, Benjamin Franklin organized the Union Fire Company, a volunteer fire-fighting unit and social society. In 1750 the Union Fire Company proposed establishing a fund "to make up the damage that may arise by fire among this company."

This idea led to the organization in 1752 of the Philadelphia Contributionship for the Insurance of Houses from Loss by Fire.[18] Franklin was among the founders of this new company, modeled on the English system of mutual insurance. Although wooden houses were accepted at first, after 1769 only brick houses within ten miles of Philadelphia were insured, and then for no more than 500 pounds. Each property was inspected and individually rated. If the house was more than two miles from the company office, the applicant for insurance had to pay the inspector's travel expenses. Policies were written for seven years, and an individual account was kept for each policyholder. By 1763, however, interest on deposited funds was pooled into a common fund for payment of losses and development of surplus.

The Contributionship applied rigorous underwriting standards. It accepted no sugar houses, brew houses, bake houses, coopers shops, or shops conducting hazardous trades such as those of apothecaries, chemists, ship-chandlers, tallow chandlers, or stable keepers. Also ineligible were buildings used to store hemp, flax, tallow, pitch, tar, turpentine, hay, straw, and fodder. When the Contributionship also refused to insure buildings with trees in front of them, the Mutual Assurance Company was formed in 1784. Because it agreed to insure such houses, this new company became known as the Green Tree Mutual.

Franklin's concern for the danger of fire continued even in the midst of his travels to London and Paris on behalf of the Colonies. Everywhere he went, he spread his ideas for preventing fires by building houses with masonry chimneys, copper roofs, and nearby water supplies. As he wrote to his daughter in 1771, "If I were to build again, I would contrive my House so as to be incapable of burning, which I think very possible and practicable."[19] Franklin's influence on his fellow Philadelphians shows in the number of brick houses built in his adopted city.

Baltimore. In 1787 the Maryland legislature chartered a stock corporation known at first as the Baltimore Insurance Fire Company and after 1791 as the Maryland Insurance Fire Company. This company also emphasized loss control. It located a powder magazine outside the town of Baltimore to reduce the hazards of gun powder explosions during conflagrations, and it organized a company to build a city water system for fire fighting purposes. A second fire insurer in Baltimore, a mutual company called the Baltimore Equitable Society, was founded in 1794. Soon after, however, the stockholders of the Maryland dissolved that company to use the capital to start two marine insurance companies.[20]

National Expansion. The Insurance Company of North America was chartered to write fire as well as marine insurance, initially providing coverage to the structure and the contents of brick and stone houses in Philadelphia. In 1797 the company decided to expand its business to Baltimore, but it needed reliable information concerning the risks to be insured. Following the example of British companies, INA sought "a person of suitable talents and integrity" in Baltimore to see that applications were in proper form, accompanied by a sketch of the property to be insured, the neighboring buildings, and a description of any extra hazards. For this service, the agent received a fee of two dollars from the applicant. Although the company feared that such local agents might sympathize more with the interests of their neighbors than with those of the insurance company, fire insurance was more profitable than marine insurance in INA's early years. In 1807 the company decided to expand its fire business into Ohio, Kentucky, Maryland, Virginia, and Tennessee by appointing local agents there. This decision ultimately spread the local agency system to the entire United States.[21]

With the rapid growth of the nation during the first half of the nineteenth century, the number of insurance companies expanded greatly. By 1824 there were at least thirty-four fire or marine insurance companies in New York, twenty in Boston, eleven in Philadelphia, and nine in Baltimore. The combined capital of these insurance companies exceeded $25 million.[22] The operations of fire insurers, however, were more often localized and concentrated in urban areas. This concentration, unfortunately, proved disastrous whenever a conflagration occurred.

Many companies were started on the assessable mutual plan under the auspices of prominent local citizens. The usual practice was to accept risks from carefully selected insureds, each of whom paid a deposit and signed a proportionate premium note for a future share in any member's losses. This assessable feature could be and often was removed as the company's surplus grew, and dividends were paid from any savings realized. The idea of banding together to provide coverage not otherwise economically available was used by farmers in 1823, by cotton-mill owners in 1835, and by lumber and hardware operators later in the same century.

New York. The growth of New York City in the early nineteenth century contributed to the development of several fire insurers in that city, starting with the United Insurance Company in 1787, the New York Insurance Company in 1798, Columbian Insurance Company in 1801, and Eagle Fire Insurance Company in 1806. The United Insurance Company of the City of New York, organized under a deed of settlement dated April 3, 1787, was the first insurance company in New York. It received a charter from the New York Legislature in 1798 permitting it to transact fire, marine, and life insurance. The authority to write property insurance extended to goods as well as buildings. In 1806 the company changed its named to the Mutual Assurance Company, and in 1809 it became a stock company. In 1846 the company took the name of the Knickerbocker Fire Insurance Company, and it continued as a major fire insurer in New York City until 1890.

Eagle Insurance Company was the first fire insurer in New York organized as a stock company. It was incorporated on April 4, 1806, with capital stock of $500,000. In 1813 Eagle transacted the first known reinsurance agreement in the United States when it assumed the entire fire insurance portfolio of the Union Insurance Company of New Jersey. Later acquired by Norwich Union Fire Insurance Society, a British insurer, Eagle became a subsidiary of Continental Insurance Companies in 1962 when Continental acquired all the American business of Norwich Union.

The great fire of 1835 was a significant setback for New York's fire insurers. On a cold December night, fire escaped from the stove of the Comstock & Andrews store on Pearl Street. With the help of a strong wind, it quickly spread to the adjoining stores and warehouses and burned for fifteen hours. It destroyed nearly 600 buildings, resulting in losses of approximately $15 million. Most New York fire insurance companies exhausted their reserves paying claims from this fire and were forced out of business. Of all the New York companies active before the fire, only three survived.

For out-of-town companies, however, the New York fire presented an opportunity. The Hartford Fire Insurance Company, founded in 1810, appointed an agent in New York in 1821, but the company did not write a single policy there until 1830. Although The Hartford had already suffered eight consecutive years of losses by 1835, it responded immediately when news of the New York fire reached Hartford. After arranging additional financing from the Hartford Bank and obtaining copies of every Hartford policy in effect in New York, the president and secretary of the company ordered a sleigh and a team of horses to carry them 108 miles through the snow to New York. They set up a temporary office to itemize, adjust, and pay claims. When discouraged New Yorkers who had purchased insurance from companies that were unable to cover their losses discovered that the Hartford paid all legitimate claims in full, many came to the temporary office to take out new policies. The Hartford Fire Insurance Company paid nearly $85,000 in claims resulting from the New York fire, but in the next six months it took in $97,000 in premiums, a five-fold increase from the year before.[23]

In 1845 another severe New York fire destroyed 450 buildings and caused the failure of still more insurers. Since most were stock companies, the mutual form of organization predominated among the new companies formed during the subsequent decades. Mutual companies, however, proved no more stable, and the possible insolvency of insurance companies was a major public concern.

New York's general insurance law of 1849 placed the licensing of new companies and the supervision of existing companies under the authority of the state controller. Each new company no longer required a specific charter from the legislature. The 1849 law also restricted each new insurance company to a single line of business so that marine insurance policyholders would not lose out because of a major fire loss and vice versa.

These new legal restrictions failed to prevent insolvencies. Of the fifty-four new companies formed following the general insurance law of 1849, forty-seven had failed by 1860, leaving unpaid losses averaging $50,000 per company.

To control this instability, New York led the way in legislating regulatory supervision over the insurance business to protect policyholders. An 1859 law established the office of Superintendent of Insurance to supervise the insurance companies operating within the state. The superintendent required insurance companies to submit financial reports and to meet certain minimum standards.

On May 9, 1867, the state legislature chartered the New York Board of Fire Underwriters to "inculcate just and equitable principles in the business of insurance, operate the Fire Patrol and assess all companies writing fire insurance in the City for maintenance of the Patrol."[24] With this authority the Board absorbed the Fire Patrol, but it also performed several other functions. For a brief period it attempted to control rates, but it abandoned this attempt in 1877 because of the frequent deviations from established rates by its members. The Board had more success in its efforts to reduce fire hazards through its inspections of buildings, arson investigations, and research into fire-fighting technology. A committee of the Board drafted the Standard Fire Policy, which the state legislature enacted in 1888 as the required form for all fire insurance policies.

National Board.   Such cooperative efforts helped to mitigate the problems facing fire insurers in the latter part of the nineteenth century. The National Board of Fire Underwriters, organized by representatives of seventy-five fire insurers in New York in 1866, attempted to maintain a uniform system of rates, establish uniform commissions, combat arson, and devise solutions to common problems. Its success in maintaining rates was uneven, but it did make progress in raising standards of fire protection in many cities. In 1874 the National Board, by threatening to suspend business in Chicago, persuaded the Chicago Citizens Association to reorganize the fire department, increase water facilities, and establish a fire marshal's bureau.

Reinsurance

As insurance companies grew, they relied increasingly on reinsurance to diversify the risks they assumed. Reinsurance, the insurance of insurance, enables insurers to spread their risks by transferring a portion of them to other insurers. This diversification is particularly helpful in avoiding excessive exposure to catastrophe losses, but the reinsurance technique serves other business purposes as well. The New York Supreme Court recognized the validity of reinsurance contracts in 1837 in the case of New York Bowery Insurance Company v. New York Fire Insurance Company.

From its earliest days, Atlantic Mutual, the oldest marine insurer in New York, maintained a reinsurance relationship with the Insurance Company of North America. This reinsurance arrangement enabled each company to write larger amounts of insurance on single ships than would otherwise be possible, because a loss would be shared with the other company.

Reinsurance was even more important for fire insurers, as the great fires of 1835 and 1846 in New York, the Chicago fire of 1871, and the Boston fire of 1872, demonstrated. Insurance companies that wrote most of their policies in the same geographic area found that they incurred losses on many of those policies simultaneously. Reinsurance enabled them to reduce their individual exposure to such catastrophes.

Many major insurance companies were based in New York City, with offices in lower Manhattan. As these primary insurance companies sought partners for reinsurance transactions, lower Manhattan became a convenient location for companies that specialized in reinsurance. The business opportunities also attracted many foreign reinsurers, such as Cologne Re and Munich Re in 1898, Skandia in 1900, and the North American Re branch of Swiss Re in 1910, that established New York offices to transact North American business. When World War I disrupted the international reinsurance market, those companies with an American branch prospered. New York thus became one of the reinsurance centers of the world.

Casualty Insurance

Marine, fire, and life insurance were the most significant types of insurance in the early years of the United States. By the middle of the nineteenth century, however, other types of insurance began to appear to meet new exposures to loss that developed as the country progressed economically.

Accident and Health Insurance. In 1850, accident and health coverage started in the United States when the Franklin Health Assurance Company of Massachusetts wrote accident insurance on travelers. Soon another company provided similar coverage and called itself The Travelers Insurance Company. Since travel was regarded as a hazard in the nineteenth century, insurance provided a measure of security to those making a trip. When Travelers founder James G. Batterson happened to meet James Bolter at the post office in 1864, he proceeded to negotiate the first policy issued by The Travelers to cover Bolter's walk home, four blocks away. The premium for this policy was two cents.[25]

Boiler Insurance. The boiler explosion at the Fales and Gray Car Works in Hartford, Connecticut, on March 2, 1854, demonstrated another danger present in an industrial society. The boiler room and surrounding buildings were completely destroyed, and twenty-one lives were lost as a result of that explosion. Determined to prevent a recurrence, several Hartford citizens formed the Polytechnic Club to apply principles of science to problems of everyday life. They soon concluded that good materials in construction, fine workmanship, careful operation, and periodic inspection would reduce the probability of boiler explosions. Following the model of the Steam Boiler Assurance Company formed in England in 1858, some members of the Polytechnic Club devised the idea of a company to inspect and insure steam boilers. The explosion of the Mississippi River steam boat Sultana on April 27, 1865, which killed 1,238 people, convinced them of the need for such a company. Many Hartford insurance men, as well as bankers and merchants, quickly subscribed the initial capital. By 1866, the Hartford Steam Boiler Inspection and Insurance Company was formed to write boiler and machinery insurance.[26]

Automobile Insurance. Other new types of insurance evolved as the needs of Americans for additional types of protection arose. The most conspicuous example was the evolution of automobile insurance, which barely existed before the twentieth century, into the largest line of insurance in the United States. The Travelers' Insurance Company issued the first automobile liability policy to Dr. Truman Martin of Buffalo, New York, in 1898. Collision coverage was first offered in 1899, and property damage coverage in 1902.

A mutual company organized in central Illinois in March 1922, State Farm Mutual Automobile Insurance Company, eventually became the largest automobile insurer in the United States and the lead company of the State Farm Group.

Workers Compensation. Another new line of business for insurers was workers compensation insurance. Under common law, workers injured in industrial accidents could sue their employers for damages. However, the employee had to prove that the employer was at fault. Employers usually argued that the employee contributed to the accident, that the employee assumed the risk of injury in accepting employment involving a known hazard, or that fellow workers rather than the employer were responsible for the injury. Because these defenses were frequently persuasive, injured workers often received no compensation at all. As the frequency of such outcomes increased, the public demand for reform also increased. New laws sought to make more employers responsible for industrial accidents. In 1887, the American Mutual Liability Company was organized to provide the new coverage required by the employer's liability law passed at that time in Massachusetts.

Helped by the anti-business sentiments spurred by revelations of life insurance improprieties, the agitation of organized labor and social reformers led to New York's enactment of the nation's first workers compensation law in 1910.[27] Since many traditional insurers supported the business community in resisting the workers compensation principle of providing compensation for work-related injuries regardless of fault, some new organizations, both private insurers and state funds, evolved to provide this new type of insurance. In time, however, many traditional insurers also began writing workers compensation insurance.

Fidelity and Surety Bonds. In 1878 the Fidelity and Casualty Company of New York began to provide fidelity and surety bonds. When in 1894 Congress passed the Heard Act, which required the bonding of government contracts, this line of business expanded dramatically. The rapid expansion of banks in the early years of the twentieth century increased the need for fidelity bonds. New companies, such as the U.S.F.&G. (founded in 1896), grew rapidly by taking advantage of the new opportunities to write fidelity and surety bonds.[28]

Life Insurance

Life insurance also developed in colonial America along the same lines as in England. The oldest life insurer in America, the Presbyterian Ministers Fund, was established in Philadelphia in 1759 to provide for the widows and children of Presbyterian ministers. Episcopal ministers organized a similar fund in 1769. Some religious sentiment, however, opposed life insurance as human interference with divine will. Other Americans regarded life insurance as a form of gambling. Still others found it difficult to put a monetary value on human life.[29] Compared to fire and marine insurance, life insurance developed slowly in the early years of the United States.

Of all forms of insurance in nineteenth century America, however, life insurance exhibited the most spectacular growth. A rash of new life insurance companies sprang up during the 1840s and 1850s, and several of those companies evolved into the giants of the industry. Examples include Mutual of New York (1843), New England Mutual (1843), Mutual Benefit (1845), New York Life (1845), State Mutual Life (1845), Connecticut Mutual (1846), Penn Mutual (1847), Union Mutual (1849), U. S. Life (1850), Aetna Life (1850), and Massachusetts Mutual (1851). Some observers attribute this burgeoning of companies to the new-found enthusiasm for marketing life insurance.[30] The dramatic growth of the life insurance business during the last half of the nineteenth century also reflected the economic transformation of the United States into an industrial power with complex financial institutions.[31] In the process companies tailored their message to emphasize the social benefits of life insurance, and agents soliciting policyholders on a person-to-person basis became an indispensable part of the business.[32]

Many of the marketing and management techniques developed by life insurance companies pervaded the entire insurance industry.[33] The size of the life insurance companies and their marketing success significantly influenced the public perception of insurance in general.

DEVELOPMENT OF INSURANCE REGULATION

Many of the current practices of the insurance business exist to satisfy certain regulatory requirements. These requirements have evolved over time in response to various public concerns. The major areas addressed by regulation have been the licensing of insurance companies, financial condition, policy language, rates, and consumer protection.

Insurance Company Licensing

After American independence, insurance companies were chartered by the individual states, which began to impose their own limitations on company activities and investments. Included was the requirement that financial statements must be submitted to state authorities periodically. Agents soliciting business in other than their domiciliary state could be required to file data about their companies, which could also be published. As early as 1824, the State of New York imposed a 10 percent tax on premiums written on New York risks by fire companies incorporated in other states, a practice followed quickly by other states. Each state zealously guarded its right to license companies and agents that wished to engage in business within its jurisdiction.

Annual Reports and Examinations

The practice of financial examination began in New York as early as 1828. In that year, New York required that an annual statement for all "monied" companies be filed with its State Comptroller. Monied companies were firms, like banks and insurance companies, that held money belonging to others. That statement required answers for thirteen categories of questions dealing with capital stock paid in; real estate, stocks, and debts of other corporations; the debts and claims against the company; the amount of insurance to which the company was bound; the losses paid in the year; the aggregate premiums and interest received; and the dividends paid on capital stock. Since the requirement was directed to all monied corporations, banks as well as insurance companies were required to file reports to ensure, in part, that proper taxes had been paid.

By 1849, New York provided for the incorporation of insurance companies by separate statute. Four years later, in 1853, a revision of the law specifically required that all companies incorporated in the state file a prescribed annual report, signed by two officers under oath. The enabling law contained three sections, one each for marine, fire, and life. This distinction was retained in subsequent legislation and imitated in other states. For this reason, United States insurance companies were generally limited to one phase of the business, while insurance companies in other areas of the world were not so restricted.

In order to forestall the problem of insolvency, states undertook to examine insurance companies, beginning with New Hampshire in 1851. By 1858, Massachusetts had two full-time examiners, Elizur Wright and George W. Sargent. The New York law of 1853 authorized the comptroller to examine any insurance company doing business in New York. This law also required insurers to maintain a reserve of sufficient funds to reinsure the unexpired terms of all outstanding policies as well as to pay all outstanding losses. In 1860, the New York State Insurance Department supplanted the State Comptroller in the regulation of insurance companies.

By 1870, many of the states had appointed a state official to oversee insurance. As early as 1865, the commissioners of Massachusetts and Connecticut appreciated the difficulties of supervising companies under the various conflicting jurisdictions and suggested federal supervision.

Standard Policies

Next to insurance company failures, the greatest bane for consumers was the complexity and difficulty of policy language, which sometimes appeared to provide a coverage in one place but then excluded it in another. Regulators and legislatures responded to this complaint by prescribing standard language for all policies written in certain lines of insurance.[34]

Life Insurance Clauses. The most stringent criticism of insurance arose in cases in which a widow did not receive the life insurance benefit she expected following her husband's death, because of a policy condition she did not understand. The less scrupulous life insurers of the time were often suspected of deliberately inserting obscure language into their policies to make them far more restrictive than their naive policyholders realized. To discourage such abuse, states enacted requirements that all life insurance policies must contain certain standard clauses.

Standard Fire Policies. During the first 100 years of its development in the United States, the fire insurance business was characterized by simple contracts written by insurers who knew their insureds well. Most insurers confined their operations to a relatively small geographical area and to insureds with whom the underwriters of the firm were familiar. Insurance was sold primarily through home office employees, without the assistance of agents or brokers. The fire insurance contract was extremely brief, including little more than the description of the property, the amount of the coverage, the period of coverage, and a premium citation. Insurance operations were characterized by individual underwriting and mutual understanding between insured and insurer. The importance of fire insurance lay not so much in the language of the agreement, the written policy, but in the mutual understanding between the parties as to what they sought to achieve.

As commerce increased and fire insurance grew into a larger, more sophisticated business, simplicity in product form and marketing methods began to bow to complexity. The prosperity experienced by commercial fire insurance brought on increased competition and more creative marketing systems. The result was a decentralization of underwriting activities, a lessening of firsthand knowledge in the selection process, and marketing through producers who often were significantly detached from the home office of the insurer.

Fire insurance companies that survived the New York fire of 1835 recognized the inherent danger of restricting operations to a limited geographical area. Consequently, they expanded their geographical underwriting boundaries. Selling and servicing policies throughout the nation proved difficult from home offices located in major cities. The property being insured, or the damage caused by each fire, was not conveniently available for examination. This difficulty led companies to pay agents in various states and towns to handle the policy sales and claims.

While such agents did alleviate some of the difficulties that distance had caused, they also introduced some new problems. An insurance company could not readily supervise the honesty of the agents or determine whether the out-of-state insurance applications contained accurate information. Moreover, the physical separation of the insured from the insurer depersonalized the insurer's relationship with its insureds and left insurers more subject to moral hazards. To alleviate these concerns, fire insurers issued policies filled with provisions designed to protect insurance companies from unwittingly accepting undesirable business and paying unjust claims.

Unfortunately, such policies became filled with restrictions, exclusions, small type, confusing sentences, and undefined terms. Insureds often found they could not collect on their policies because of unseen exclusions buried deep in the fine print. Insurers found it hard to negotiate claim settlements because their policy conditions had become nullified, or otherwise modified, by widely differing court decisions. As stated in a court decision of 1873:

> Forms of applications and policies . . . of a most complicated and elaborate structure, were prepared, and filled with covenants, exceptions, stipulations, provisos, rules, regulations and conditions, rendering the policy void in a great number of contingencies. . . . Some of the most material stipulations were concealed in a mass of rubbish on the back side of the policy and the following page, where few would expect to find anything more than a dull appendix, . . . As if it were feared that . . . some extremely eccentric person might attempt to examine and understand the meaning of the involved and intricate net in which he was to be entangled—it was printed in such small type and in lines so long and so crowded that the perusal of it was made physically

difficult, painful and injurious. Seldom has the art of typography been so successfully diverted from the diffusion of knowledge to the suppression of it. There was ground for the premium payer to argue that the print alone was evidence . . . of a fraudulent plot.[35]

Lack of Uniformity. As fire insurance developed in the 1800s, individual insurers went their own ways in developing customized fire insurance contracts. Product competition and customization led to a "hodge-podge" of fire insurance contracts, which resulted in consumer confusion. Fire insurance became an enigma to many insureds, and the insurance industry was increasingly viewed with suspicion.

The absence of standard wording among fire insurance contracts gave rise to numerous problems both for insureds and insurers. Consumers knew what they thought the agreement was supposed to do. However, most consumers had not studied the policy in detail and were not at all certain of the implications of all of its provisions. At the same time, with insurers developing their own contracts without reference to any common wording, fire insurance contracts were too often ambiguous. Problems arose in the interpretation of coverage, resulting in litigation and settlement of loss where dual coverage existed. It became apparent that uniformity was a desirable goal.

Contract Standardization. The first serious attempt to develop a standard policy is believed to have been undertaken by the National Board of Fire Underwriters in 1868. Massachusetts adopted a standard form for the writing of fire insurance in 1873, followed by Michigan in 1881 and New Hampshire in 1885. The New York legislature adopted a standard policy in 1887. This policy was the result of collaboration within the insurance industry. While formerly designated the "General Standard Fire Policy," it was popularly known as the "1886 form" (even though it was adopted in 1887).

In 1916, the National Convention of Insurance Commissioners (now the National Association of Insurance Commissioners), following several years of deliberation, recommended a new standard form. This new form significantly decreased the number of clauses found in the "1886 form" that dealt with moral hazard. The old form contained "if clauses," which voided coverage once a violation occurred. The new form substituted "while clauses," which had the effect of temporarily suspending coverage under certain circumstances. Other changes also were recommended and, in 1918, New York adopted the resulting "200 line form," which became known as the "Commissioners' form."

The 1943 New York Standard Fire Policy. In 1936, a committee of the National Association of Insurance Commissioners recommended revision of the 1918 form. Recommended changes in the policy included (1) adding lightning and fire caused by riot as perils covered, (2) modifying the policy to an "interest" contract covering to the extent of the policyholder's insurable interest rather than requiring that the insured be the sole and unconditional owner of the property in order to have coverage, (3) allowing of assignment of the policy with the insurer's consent, (4) liberalizing vacancy and unoccupancy clauses to allow such conditions if for less than sixty days, and (5) stipulating that in the event of loss (and multiple coverage) the loss would be prorated among insurers according to the face amounts of the coverage, whether collectible or not. On July 1, 1943, New York adopted this "165 line form," popularly known as the New York Standard Fire Policy, or simply the standard fire policy. In most states the 1943 New York Standard Fire Policy was "approved" by reference in the insurance code of the state or by insurance department regulation, but some states incorporated the exact wording of the policy into a statute. This standard policy language was required in any fire insurance policy, but most states have now abandoned this requirement.

Rate Regulation

Rate regulation was largely unheard of until nearly the end of the nineteenth century. Prior to that time, insurance was considered simply a private contract, the terms of which grew out of the negotiations between the parties. If one party or the other did not like the price, he did not make the contract. The free market, not the government, determined prices.

That attitude in American society underwent a fundamental transformation during the period roughly from 1887 to 1916. During those years, major legislation, such as the Interstate Commerce Act, the Sherman Act, the Clayton Act, and the Federal Reserve Act, reflected a new business climate in the United States and a new role for the government. The controversies of that time influenced the structure of the insurance business as much as any other business in the United States.

The fundamental political question of the time was what to do about the "trusts."[36] In the vocabulary of the time, trusts were combinations of business firms that attempted to dominate the market and control prices. The leading example was the Standard Oil Trust established in 1879, which combined the property of over forty petroleum refining and pipeline firms, representing 90 percent of the industry. The resulting market power of such combinations prompted consumer rebellions that spilled over into politics. Consumer resentment was particularly strong in the South and Midwest, where the trusts were often perceived as controlled by Eastern interests. The *Omaha Herald,* for example, advised its readers that "The West should drop political lines and vote as a unit for the man of its choice, and thus serve notice upon the Eastern capitalistic and monopoly element that it cannot run the country."[37]

While regional sentiments were significant, more important was the shifting economic balance of power. The growth of large corporations meant that business transactions were no longer the outcome of bargaining between equal parties. Midwestern farmers, for example, were at the mercy of freight rates set by the major railroads and credit terms set by banks. The growing concentration of economic power caused consumers to turn to the political arena to redress the balance. The Northwestern Alliance, a farmers' organization that sponsored cooperative ventures such as stores, grain elevators, and insurance companies, sent two of its leaders to the United States Senate. According to one of them, Senator William Peffer of Kansas, the Alliance represented a defensive movement against "the most powerful and active agencies in modern civilization, whose work is clearly traceable in our recent history—railroads, middlemen, and banks."[38]

Anti-Trust Laws. The apparent remedy to this abuse of economic power was to outlaw collusion or conspiracy in restraint of trade. Several states passed "anti-trust" laws intended to prohibit economic combinations that restrained trade and diminished competition. In 1890 the U.S. Congress followed suit by enacting the Sherman Antitrust Act. Insurance consumers hoped that these state and federal antitrust laws would limit the ability of insurers to raise rates, but the application of antitrust laws to insurance proved complicated.

Rate Regulation. An alternative method of preventing big corporations from abusing their economic power is to regulate prices. Several Midwestern states passed laws in the 1870s regulating the rates charged by railroads and other private firms. These laws were challenged and were eventually appealed to the United States Supreme Court. In the most famous case, Munn v. Illinois, the Supreme Court upheld the power of a state to regulate the rates charged by private businesses, whether corporations or unincorporated firms like the Munn & Scott grain elevator, provided the regulated market was "affected with the public interest." According to this decision, when "one devotes his property to a use in which the public has an interest, he, in effect, grants to the public an interest in that use, and must submit to be controlled by the public for the common good."[39] The result of this decision was a distinct set of legal principles for quasi-public or public service companies. These firms, unlike corporations in general, had an obligation to provide universal service and uphold the public interest in other ways.[40]

Rating Bureaus. Another approach favored in some states was to promote industry control of rates through the formation of rating bureaus. In practice, insurance rates were probably never determined in an entirely free market. When competition did exist, insurers cut prices to levels that could not support severe losses. Catastrophes wiped out many insurance companies. Insurers frequently tried to organize the market to control rates and break this devastating cycle.

The normal practice was to devise a rate "tariff" listing the prescribed rates for different classes of risks. Insurers agreed to abide by the tariff, which their agents carried with them as they solicited business. In time, loss statistics helped to refine the tariffs to reflect the degree of risk inherent in the various classes of business.

An early example of a rating bureau was the Ohio Inspection Bureau, organized by T. B. Sellers, whose brother later formed a similar organization in Indiana. These bureaus were privately owned, frequently by a single person, to avoid state antitrust laws. Eventually state restrictions were removed, and a fire insurance rating bureau was established in every state. The need for uniform approaches to ratemaking and form language led to regional advisory organizations, which eventually took control of the local bureaus in their regions. In 1960 these organizations were consolidated into the Inter-Regional Insurance Conference, later the Fire Insurance Research and Actuarial Association, and they eventually became part of the Insurance Services Office. In addition to the fire rate bureaus, separate rating bureaus developed for inland marine, casualty, surety, workers compensation, and multiple-line insurance.

Legislative Investigations. Public dissatisfaction with certain insurance practices led to legislative investigations, such as those conducted in New York by the Armstrong and Merritt Committees.

Armstrong Committee. In 1905, a New York Legislative Committee (the "Armstrong Committee") undertook an extensive investigation of life insurance companies, especially those issuing deferred-dividend policies. The committee found extravagance in agents' commissions, officers' salaries, and lobbying expenses. Control of company officers' authority was found lacking, and home offices had become extravagant and lavish. Investment in stocks of banks had weakened the financial strength of many insurance companies. Extensive changes affecting life insurance companies were enacted in New York. These changes included requiring consent of the Superintendent of Insurance before real estate for company use could be acquired, the reporting of officer salaries over $5,000, the limiting of commissions, and the allocating of dividends annually. Other states also required the listing of all officer salaries and the use of a voucher system of payment.

Merritt Committee. A similar legislative committee, with Edwin A. Merritt as chairman, was organized on July 8, 1910, to investigate fire insurance, as well as cases of legislative influence peddling involving a stock broker and a race track. The Merritt Committee held hearings at New York City Hall and heard 117 witnesses describe the practices of fire insurers. Although many complained about arbitrary rate increases, the committee found no scandals such as those revealed by the Armstrong Committee. Instead, the committee suggested the licensing of agents, the admission of miscellaneous mutual companies, and a prohibition against rebating.

With regard to rates, the committee praised the practice of schedule rating, which the rating bureaus had developed to charge lower rates for buildings with sprinklers or various other construction features that reduced the probability of fire losses. Schedule rating, however, required insurers to cooperate through the rating bureaus. Therefore, the committee declared: "Our conclusion then is that combination and equity in rates should be inseparable."[41] This conclusion justified state intervention into the market to facilitate schedule rating. The legislature responded with a rating law in 1911 that authorized four rating bureaus to operate in New York state, provided that they disclosed their procedures and submitted to examination by the State Insurance Department.

Kansas Rate Law. Consumer complaints regarding rating inequities in Kansas led to a different outcome when that state's Superintendent of Insurance, Charles W. Barnes, proposed a rate control law in 1909. Barnes believed that the state's arguments with fire insurers over their alleged violations of the antitrust law had been a waste of time. "Reasonable rates cannot be guaranteed with this kind of legislation," he said. Instead the government should intervene directly. "If the State Board of Railroad Commissioners can fix freight and passenger rates, I see no reason why this department should not be authorized to fix insurance rates."[42] Kansas already regulated not only railroads, but all common carriers, and a law passed in 1905 subjected petroleum pipelines to such regulation as well.

The Kansas legislature agreed with Superintendent Barnes. The rate control law took effect on June 1, 1909, but the insurance companies regarded it as drastic interference with their private business. The German Alliance Insurance Company brought suit in federal court to block enforcement of the law. The court sustained the law, finding no conflict with either the Kansas or the United States Constitution. The case was ultimately appealed to the Supreme Court, which upheld the law in 1914. Since insurance was "a business affected with the public interest," as construed in the Munn v. Illinois decision, the Court concluded that rate regulation was an appropriate function of government.[43]

The Supreme Court's conclusion in this case is the basis for government regulation of all aspects of the insurance business. In the words of the Wisconsin insurance commissioner, the decision "changes the whole status of the business. . . . It has elevated this to a place of importance alongside the railroad and other great quasi-public enterprises."[44]

New York Rate Law of 1922. New York applied the power of rate regulation with equal vigor, but with a different approach. New York's first rate law in 1911 required fire insurers to join one of the four approved rating bureaus, whose methods and operations were subject to examination by the Insurance Department. It also prohibited discriminatory rates. Another legislative investigation, the Lockwood Committee, confirmed the existence of continued inequities. As a result, the New York Rate Law of 1922 required the New York Insurance Department to regulate rates of all insurance lines except life, marine, and accident and health. The Insurance Department attempted to determine that rates were reasonable; that is, neither excessive nor inadequate. For this purpose, casualty insurance companies in New York were required by the Insurance Department in 1923 to file a Casualty Experience Exhibit.

In a 1925 noninsurance case, the U.S. Supreme Court affirmed that in certain areas, public policy favors the exchange of cost and pricing information in a competitive environment:

> The public interest is served by the gathering and dissemination, in the widest possible manner, of information with respect to the production and distribution, cost and prices in actual sales of market commodities, because the making available of such information tends to stabilize trade and industry, to produce fairer price levels and to avoid the waste which inevitably attends the unintelligent conduct of economic enterprise.[45]

With this blessing, states continued to expand their regulation of insurance rates, and rating bureaus became the preferred way to gather the necessary information. The bureaus imposed considerable structure on the industry. For example, the rules of the New York Fire Insurance Exchange restricted member companies to just one agent in Manhattan and the Bronx, regulated the rates charged and the commissions paid to agents and subagents, and required that all policies be paid or canceled by the twentieth of the second month following the inception of the policy. The Exchange audited agents' records and imposed fines for violations.

However, the variation from one company to another in expenses concerned many insurance commissioners and prompted further attempts to collect relevant information. In 1935, New York required an expense exhibit of fire and marine companies similar to the casualty experience expense exhibit. These reports were to be made by line of coverage. As only limited instructions were initially presented on accounting for costs, the companies gradually developed their own approaches, using the suggestions of actuaries and accountants.

Challenge to State Regulation

The Supreme Court's decision in 1914 established the power of the government to regulate insurance rates. The only remaining question was which level of government should exercise that power. This question, moreover, was complicated by confusion surrounding the Supreme Court decision in Paul v. Virginia and the regulatory processes already established.

Paul v. Virginia. From 1869 until 1944 the misconstrued precedent of the Paul v. Virginia case dominated insurance regulation. The case stemmed from the legislation enacted in Virginia in 1866 requiring licenses for out-of-state insurance companies. Licenses were granted only to those companies that deposited bonds with the state treasurer in excess of $30,000. Another law required licenses for any person acting as an agent of an out-of-state insurance company.

Several New York companies appointed as their agent in Virginia a Petersburg attorney named Samuel D. Paul, who was determined to test the constitutionality of the law. Paul applied for a license, which was denied because the companies he represented had not deposited the required bonds with the state treasurer. When Paul continued to write business for the New York companies, he was indicted, convicted, and fined. The case of Paul v. Virginia was eventually appealed to the United States Supreme Court.

The argument presented on Paul's behalf asserted that the Virginia law was unconstitutional because it interfered with the federal government's power to regulate interstate commerce. The Supreme Court rejected that argument and upheld the Virginia law. The court's unanimous opinion, delivered by Chief Justice Stephen J. Field, concluded in Paul's favor:

> Issuing a policy of insurance is not a transaction of commerce. The policies are simple contracts of indemnity against loss by fire. . . . They are not commodities to be shipped or forwarded from one State to another, and then put up for sale. They are like other personal contracts between parties which are completed by their signature and the transfer of the consideration. . . . The policies do not take effect—are not executed contracts—until delivered by the agent in Virginia. They are, then, local transactions, governed by local law.[46]

While the effect of this decision was to uphold the regulation of the insurance business by the state of Virginia, over the next seventy-five years Field's words were often cited to oppose federal regulation of insurance. The argument that insurance was not commerce prevailed until 1944, when the Supreme Court explicitly affirmed the federal power to regulate insurance.

Federal Initiatives. Although state regulation grew in the years following the Paul v. Virginia decision, some thought it was not sufficient. In the aftermath of the Armstrong Investigation, many voices advocated federal regulation of insurance. Some were the critics of the insurance companies, who wanted to control the perceived abuses. Other voices, however, came from within the industry. U.S. Senator John F. Dryden of New Jersey, also president of Prudential Life, proposed federal regulation in 1905 because he considered it "infinitely preferable to the intolerable supervision" of fifty state insurance departments. In his annual message to Congress that December, President Theodore Roosevelt proposed that the insurance business should be supervised and regulated by the Bureau of Corporations, but Congress did not act on this proposal.

Southeastern Underwriters Case. The Missouri rate law served to frustrate insurance consumers and commissioners throughout the 1920s and 1930s. Every time the Commissioner rejected a rate filing, the industry appealed to the state court, leaving the proposed rates in effect while the case was pending. The insurers collected the full rate, but the disputed amount was deposited with court appointed custodians. Disputed Missouri rate cases between 1922 and 1941 created a custodial fund of about nine million dollars.

The Missouri Attorney General, Roy McKittrick, eventually persuaded the federal government to challenge the rating bureaus under the antitrust laws. The Attorney General of the United States, Francis Biddle, convinced of the dangers of economic concentration by the hearings of the Temporary National Economic Committee, launched an investigation of the insurance industry. In 1942 the Justice Department charged the Southeastern Underwriters Association (SEUA) and nine of its member insurance companies with violations of the Sherman Antitrust Act. The SEUA was a rating bureau in Atlanta owned by 200 private stock fire insurers. According to the indictment, these companies controlled more than 90 percent of the fire insurance business written in the six states of Alabama, Florida, Georgia, North Carolina, South Carolina, and Virginia.

The case was ultimately appealed to the Supreme Court, which stunned the industry in 1944 with its finding that the Southeastern Underwriters had violated the antitrust laws.

The old dilemma of state or federal regulation was no longer a constitutional question. To the question of which level of government had the power to regulate insurance, the Supreme Court answered "both." Thus the issue came down to an economic question, what type of regulation is most effective?

McCarran-Ferguson Act. The decision in the Southeastern Underwriters case left the regulation of the insurance business in doubt. The Roosevelt Administration promised not to allow any sudden changes while the Congress deliberated on the solution to the dilemma. The National Association of Insurance Commissioners proposed legislation that would coordinate state and federal antitrust law regarding the insurance business.[47] This legislation was essentially a federalist solution to the question because it preserved the structure of existing state regulation while explicitly placing the insurance business under ultimate federal authority.

This federalist solution was achieved by the language of the law's exemption of the insurance business from the Sherman, Clayton, and Federal Trade Commission Acts to the extent that it is regulated by the states. However, the law also provided that the federal antitrust laws do apply in cases of boycott, coercion, or intimidation. The text of the Act appears in Exhibit 1-1.

All-Industry Bill. Following passage of the McCarran-Ferguson Act, the NAIC held extensive hearings to determine the best framework for state regulation. Under the leadership of New York Superintendent Robert Dineen, the hearings resulted in proposed legislation called the All-Industry Bill, and in 1946 the NAIC adopted it as a model law. According to the All-Industry Bill:

> The commissioner shall promulgate reasonable rules and statistical plans, reasonably adapted to each of the rating systems on file with him which may be modified from time to time and which shall be used thereafter by each insurer in the recording and reporting of its loss, and countrywide expense experiences, in order that the experience of all insurers may be made available at least annually in such form and detail as may be necessary to aid him in determining whether rating systems comply with the standards set forth....[48]

This development prompted the formation of the National Association of Independent Insurers (NAII) to assert the position of companies like State Farm and Allstate that preferred open competition in rates.[49] The goals of the NAII were to preserve the independence of its members from the bureaus, to permit deviations from the bureau rates, and to facilitate reporting statistical data in a manner consistent with the rating systems of its members.

The forces for rigid rate regulation were stronger, however. By 1948 every state enacted a rate regulatory law, usually patterned after the All-Industry Bill, to meet the provision of the McCarran-Ferguson Act exempting insurance from the federal antitrust laws. Although these state laws vary in their details, all of them provide for the supervision and proper control of the insurance ratemaking process. In most states these laws served to entrench the rating bureaus, provided that

Exhibit 1-1
Text of the McCarran-Ferguson Act

McCarran-Ferguson Act 15 U.S.C.
Sections 1011-1015 March 9, 1945

Section 1011.

The Congress hereby declares that the continued regulation and taxation by the several States of the business of insurance is in the public interest, and that silence on the part of the Congress shall not be construed to impose any barrier to the regulation or taxation of such business by the several States.

Section 1012.

(a) The business of insurance, and every person engaged therein, shall be subject to the laws of the several States which relate to the regulation or taxation of such business.

(b) No act of Congress shall be construed to invalidate, impair, or supersede any law enacted by any State for the purpose of regulating the business of insurance, or which imposes a fee or a tax upon such business, unless such Act specifically relates to the business of insurance: Provided, That after June 30, 1948, the Act of July 2, 1890, as amended, known as the Sherman Act, and the Act of October 15, 1914, as amended, known as the Clayton Act, and the Act of September 26, 1914, known as the Federal Trade Commission Act, as amended, shall be applicable to the business of insurance to the extent that such business is not regulated by State law.

Section 1013.

(a) Until July 30, 1948, the Act of July 2, 1890, as amended, known as the Sherman Act, and the Act of October 15, 1914, as amended, known as the Clayton Act, and the Act of September 26, 1914, known as the Federal Trade Commission Act, as amended, and the Act of June 19, 1936, known as the Robinson-Patman Antidiscrimination Act, shall not apply to the business of insurance or to acts in the conduct thereof.

(b) Nothing contained in this Act shall render the said Sherman Act inapplicable to any agreement to boycott, coerce, or intimidate, or act of boycott, coercion, or intimidation.

Section 1014.

Nothing contained in this Act shall be construed to affect in any manner the application to the business of insurance of the Act of July 5, 1935, as amended, known as the National Labor Relations Act, or the Act of June 25, 1938, as amended, known as the Fair Labor Standards Act of 1938, or the Act of June 5, 1920, known as the Merchant Marine Act, 1920.

Section 1015.

As used in this Act, the term "State" includes the several States, Alaska, Hawaii, Puerto Rico, Guam, and the District of Columbia.

they shed the trade association functions some had performed as well. Thus it could be said that the New York solution rather than the Kansas solution to the problem of rate regulation prevailed for most of the twentieth century.

In this environment, bureau-made rates were the order of the day, and deviations and independent filings the infrequent exceptions. The additional expense required to justify rate deviations created barriers to competition, and regulators were not necessarily sympathetic. Some companies, such as INA and State Farm, fought for the right to make independent filings, but the rating bureaus countered most of their efforts. Reflecting on the contentious rate hearings and legal challenges of the 1950s, INA's assistant counsel, William B. Pugh, Jr., commented that "The bureau companies woke up to the fact that their chief accomplishment had been to encase themselves in a regulatory straitjacket while the independents walked off with the business."[50]

Separation of Lines

As new lines of insurance evolved, the separation of different lines became increasingly important to regulators. Their evaluation of rates and the adequacy of reserves depended on the examination of distinct lines of business. At the first meeting of the National Convention of Insurance Commissioners in 1871, New York's Superintendent of Insurance suggested that life insurance companies should not be allowed to write any accident or casualty insurance.[51] Most states followed New York's example, and their corporation laws restricted the underwriting authority of insurance companies. When a new company applied for a corporate charter, it had to specify whether its business would be fire, marine, or life insurance. Casualty insurance emerged during the nineteenth century as a fourth category, including many new types of insurance. The limited scope of insurance company charters not only separated life insurance from other forms of insurance, but also precluded any single insurer from writing both property and casualty insurance. One significant outgrowth was the extreme compartmentalization of the American insurance business, compared to practices elsewhere in the world. To surmount these restrictions, American insurers organized groups, or "fleets," of companies writing different lines but owned in common.

According to the most thorough study of this subject, there were two objectives in the minds of those who created the restrictions on underwriting powers:

> It was designed, first, to permit individual insurers to specialize in the extremely technical problems of particular kinds of insurance and thus develop proficiency and safety in the treatment of specified haz-

ards. This specialization undoubtedly was presumed, at the time, to be in the best interests of the insuring public.

Second, it was felt desirable to segregate the classes of insurance so that a more accurate appraisal could be made of the financial qualifications to be demanded of insurers, to the end that regulatory requirements could be specifically established by state supervisory officials which would fit the peculiar conditions prevailing in different phases of the insurance business.[52]

Appelton Rule. The New York insurance law limited a particular insurer to underwriting either fire and marine, or casualty and surety lines. Other states were less stringent, but New York practice prevailed nationwide because of the so-called Appelton rule. Promulgated by Deputy Superintendent of Insurance H. D. Appelton, this rule required all insurers licensed in New York state to accept the New York limitations on their underwriting powers wherever they operated. Since most major insurers wanted to operate in New York, they were forced to accept this separation of lines. In 1940, the Appelton Rule was explicitly incorporated into the insurance law of New York.

Nation-Wide Marine Definition. Another line of insurance, inland marine, developed rapidly in the early part of the twentieth century. New modes of transportation and new types of personal property created new exposures not suited to insurance under the conventional fire or casualty forms. Marine insurers, being relatively unconstrained by regulation of rates and contracts, grew rapidly by offering insurance on goods in transit, jewelry, fur coats, fine arts, cameras, musical instruments, jewelers' inventories, bridges and tunnels, and other classes of property under marine forms.

In 1932, however, New York limited the types of property eligible for insurance under a marine policy. The following year the National Convention of Insurance Commissioners adopted a "Nation-Wide Definition and Interpretation of the Insuring Powers of Marine and Transportation Underwriters." This definition, eventually adopted by a majority of the states, specified in some detail what exposures could and could not be covered by marine insurance. Exposures that could not be covered by marine insurers were insured by fire or casualty insurers. Although uninsured gaps remained, fire and casualty insurers were somewhat successful in limiting the further expansion of marine underwriters. A committee of insurance company representatives was empowered by regulations in many states and by agreements among insurance companies to penalize insurers writing business as marine insurance that was outside the Nation-Wide Definition.

Multiple-Line Insurance. Among the leading critics of the Appelton Rule was the long-time chief executive of Atlantic Mutual, William D. Winter, also the author of a well-known text on marine insurance. In Winter's opinion, the result of the limited scope of underwriting authority was that "the fire, marine, and the rapidly growing casualty and automobile sections of the insurance business have been developed as entirely independent enterprises, staffed in the same company or group by separate internal organizations, each jealous of its own position in its own company organization and in the insurance business as a whole."[53]

A second consequence, in Winter's opinion, was that the Appelton Rule "tended to create a vacuum in the insurance business where serious hazards could find no protection under American insurance . . . [and] in many cases went for protection to foreign insurance markets."[54]

Winter served on the Multiple Line Committee of Eight appointed by the National Association of Insurance Commissioners in 1943. The committee, chaired by John A. Diemand of INA, represented a cross-section of the industry. The committee met every Wednesday in the Johnson & Higgins board room in New York to study the many coverage gaps that existed in the modern insurance world.

One problem studied by the Committee of Eight was the comprehensive automobile policy. Winter explained the problem as follows:

> Under the Appelton Rule fire companies could insure the automobile, casualty companies the third party liabilities that arose out of its ownership and use, and in between was a no man's land where the boundaries were not too well defined. In the case of the automobile, the need for all risks coverage became so insistent that something had to be done about it, and the system evolved of having a complete policy written by two companies, often on the same sheet of paper. This made necessary the formation of group underwriting, where a fire company would organize or buy a casualty company or vice versa. Thus by this rather unbusinesslike device a single policy could be issued and a single financial source, although in two company parts, could be offered for the protection and convenience of the assured and the agent."[55]

The final report of the Diemand Committee recommended that fire, marine, casualty, and surety companies be permitted to write any kind of insurance except life outside the United States and to accept reinsurance for the same lines within the United States. It also recommended authorizing insurers to write comprehensive automobile policies, comprehensive aviation policies, and personal property floaters. Although these recommendations met considerable opposition from the industry, the NAIC adopted them in June 1944 and referred them to the states.

In 1949 a new law in New York authorized full underwriting powers to both fire and marine, and casualty and surety insurers. This New York law was the turning point, for all other states enacted similar legislation within a few years if they did not already permit multiple-line underwriting.[56] This change enabled insurers to operate as multiple-line companies and to combine different types of coverage into a single policy. Many small companies that wrote only one line became obsolete as a result.

Consumerism

During the latter half of the nineteenth century, several major companies in the New York area grew rapidly and dominated the life insurance business of the United States. The same dominance did not prevail in property and liability insurance despite the presence of many major companies in New York. While life insurers were active investors in New York capital markets, property and liability insurers emphasized investment operations less and underwriting operations more. Thus it was more advantageous for them to be located closer to the risks they underwrote. Midwestern resentment of Eastern financiers also spawned many local and regional insurance companies in late nineteenth-century America, and New York companies often found it difficult to compete against them on their home ground. Many states also levied premium taxes on out-of-state insurers, adding to the disadvantage faced by New York insurers.

Such regional sentiments were exacerbated by the findings of the Armstrong Committee in 1905 and the Merritt Committee in 1910. The Armstrong investigations revealed significant abuses by major life insurers. The Merritt Committee focused on the rating practices of fire insurers. That subject had become controversial because New York fire rates, which had been generally lower in New York than elsewhere, rose sharply during the 1890s and 1900s.

Thus the fundamental issue that excited consumers involved the appropriate rates. Rates that are adequate, but not excessive, are difficult to determine precisely and often subject to contention. Regardless of the particular rating law in force, this problem has been at the heart of consumer unrest throughout the twentieth century. High rates lead to consumer protest, but low rates lead to insurer insolvency. Consumers lose either way, and both possibilities are as likely in the 1990s as they were in the 1890s.

As the size of insurance companies has grown, however, so has the problem of insolvency. In 1947 New York enacted an insurance "guaranty fund" law, which assesses all insurers a percentage of premiums written for the guaranty fund, which pays the unsatisfied claims against insolvent insurance companies. All other states followed suit with guaranty funds of their own. The guaranty fund mechanism has been severely tested, and critics contend not only that its operations are cumbersome in the event of an insolvency, but also that it penalizes prudent insurers in order to redress the failures of their less responsible competitors.

In the late 1960s and continuing through the 1970s and 1980s, many states replaced their prior approval law with some type of open competition law for the reasons discussed previously. In 1987, various types of competitive rating laws were in operation in thirty-six states.[57] In some states, rates for certain lines of insurance are still subject to prior approval by state insurance regulators, while rates for other lines can be determined by competition. More recently, there has been a movement away from open competition laws back toward stringent rate regulation. In a number of states, insurers have even been required to roll back rates. For example, passage of Proposition 103 in California on November 28, 1988, required insurers to reduce most insurance rates 20 percent below the level that existed on November 8, 1987. Good drivers would be eligible for an additional discount of 20 percent. In Pennsylvania, a consumer choice law was enacted recently that required insurers to roll back auto insurance rates 22 percent for insureds who elected a verbal threshold for lawsuits and 10 percent for insureds who elected to retain the existing tort-liability based system. In Arizona, a proposal for a prior approval law was recently defeated. Similar efforts to reduce auto insurance rates have occurred in other states, and many are being appealed in the courts.

The movement away from open competition rating laws can be explained, at least partly, by the widespread public belief that insurance rates, primarily auto insurance rates, are prohibitively high, and that insurers are earning excessive profits. However, auto insurers argue that rates are high in certain states because of high claim costs and not excessive rates. Claim costs are high in these states because of the large number of cars and auto accidents, defects in the legal system, inflation of medical costs, fraud, and numerous other factors.

Consumer protection and solvency have required regulators to innovate increasingly sophisticated methods for supervising a complex business. At the same time, regulation has evolved into a significant political issue for American society.

SUMMARY

Insurance evolved to satisfy the risk bearing needs of society. As trade, shipping, and credit facilities appeared in medieval Europe, insurance facilities appeared as well. Not by accident, the Italian cities and Antwerp, Amsterdam, and London in time served as insurance, financial, and commercial centers. These centers were known both for the facilities they offered for all of these commercial needs and the government sanctions that assured the enforcement of contracts.

By the end of the eighteenth century, London had surpassed the other insurance markets of the world, and British insurance practice had been transplanted throughout the British Empire. Thus insurance in the United States developed from its colonial heritage. As the country grew, however, insurance evolved to adapt to new situations. Marine insurers found a new opportunity when the country became independent, but their fortunes always followed those of American shippers. Fire insurance became a major business in nineteenth-century America as buildings mushroomed everywhere across a growing country. New lines of insurance, including accident, boiler and machinery, automobile, workers compensation, and surety, emerged to meet new types of risks. Although of little importance in the early history of the United States, by the end of the nineteenth century the spectacular growth of life insurance companies turned them into dominant financial institutions with considerable influence on the practice, regulation, and public perception of other types of insurance as well.

If the variety and vitality of separate lines is one distinctive characteristic of the American insurance business, the nature and extent of its regulation is another. Regulation has shaped the evolution of the business in the United States from its earliest days. In an economy based on private property and free enterprise, new firms and new techniques were constantly evolving, but not all were successful. Thus government authorities intervened, attempting to regulate the solvency of insurance companies. When apparent abuses seemed to demand it, regulation of rates and contracts followed. Some interests advocate more effective state regulation of insurance, others advocate federal regulation, but in a competitive economy the basic tension between free enterprise and consumer protection is ever present.

Chapter Notes

1. Donald McCloskey, *Prosperous Peasants* (Princeton, NJ: Princeton University Press, 1992).
2. Irving Pfeffer, "The Early History of Insurance," *The Annals of The Society of Chartered Property and Casualty Underwriters*, vol. 19 (Summer 1966), pp. 101-112.
3. David Hughes, *A Treatise on the Law Related to Insurance in These Parts* (O. Halstead, Collins and Hannay, and Gould and Banks; Grigg and Elliot, 1833), p. 342.
4. Letter dated March 13, 1400, quoted by Florence Elder de Roover, "Early Examples of Marine Insurance," *Journal of Economic History*, vol. V (November 1945), p. 197.
5. Jonathan I. Israel, *Dutch Primacy in World Trade, 1585-1740* (Oxford: Oxford University Press, 1989), pp. 21-22.
6. Hermann van der Wee, "Money, Credit and Banking Systems," *The Cambridge Economic History of Europe*, vol. V (Cambridge: Cambridge University Press, 1977), pp. 337-338.
7. Frank C. Spooner, *Risks at Sea: Amsterdam Insurance and Maritime Europe, 1766-1780* (Cambridge: Cambridge University Press, 1983), pp. 17-21.
8. Stephen M. Stigler, *The History of Statistics: The Measurement of Uncertainty before 1900* (Cambridge, MA: Harvard University Press, 1986), p. 4.
9. James D. Tracy, *A Financial Revolution in the Hapsburg Netherlands* (Berkeley, CA: University of California Press, 1985), pp. 210-213.
10. Stigler, p. 65.
11. Robin Pearson, "Thrift or Dissipation? The Business of Life Assurance in the Early Nineteenth Century," *The Economic History Review*, vol. XLIII (May 1990), pp. 236-254.
12. Thomas M. Doerflinger, *A Vigorous Spirit of Enterprise: Merchants and Economic Development in Revolutionary Philadelphia* (Chapel Hill, NC: University of North Carolina Press, 1986), pp. 47-48. Eugene R. Slaski, "Thomas Willing: Moderation during the American Revolution" (Ph.D. dissertation, Florida State University, 1971), p. 43.
13. Bernard L. Webb, "Notes on the Early History of American Insurance," *The Annals of The Society of Chartered Property and Casualty Underwriters*, vol. 29 (June 1976), pp. 92-93.
14. "An Early Fire Insurance Company," *South Carolina Historical and Genealogical Magazine* (January 1907), pp. 46-53.
15. *The Papers of Benjamin Franklin* (New Haven and London: Yale University Press, 1960-1974), vol. 3, pp. 257-258.
16. I. Bernard Cohen, *Benjamin Franklin: His Contribution to the American Tradition* (Indianapolis and New York: The Bobbs-Merrill Company, 1953), pp. 189-205.

17. The Pennsylvania Gazette, February 4, 1734, *The Papers of Benjamin Franklin*, vol. 2, p. 12.
18. Deed of Settlement, March 25, 1752, *The Papers of Benjamin Franklin*, vol. 4, pp. 281-295. Nicholas B. Wainwright, *A Philadelphia Story: The Philadelphia Contributionship for the Insurance of Houses from Loss by Fire* (Philadelphia, 1952), pp. 21-28.
19. Letter to Deborah Franklin, July 4, 1771, *The Papers of Benjamin Franklin*, vol. 18, p. 161.
20. Webb, p. 93.
21. Marquis James, *Biography of a Business: Insurance Company of North America, 1792-1943* (Indianapolis, IN: The Bobbs-Merrill Company, 1942), pp. 96-104.
22. Herman E. Krooss, "Financial Institutions," *The Growth of the Seaport Cities, 1790-1825*, edited by David T. Gilchrist (Charlottesville, VA: The University Press of Virginia, 1967), pp. 108-109.
23. Hawthorne Daniel, *The Hartford of Hartford* (New York: Random House, 1960), pp. 61-75.
24. *The New York Board of Fire Underwriters, 1867-1967* (New York: New York Board of Fire Underwriters, 1967), p. 10.
25. *The Travelers 100 Years* (Hartford, CT: The Travelers, 1964), p. 1.
26. Glenn Weaver, *The Hartford Steam Boiler Inspection and Insurance Company* (Hartford, CT, 1966) pp. 3-11.
27. Robert Asher, "Failure and Fulfillment: Agitation for Employers' Liability Legislation and the Origins of Workmen's Compensation in New York State, 1876-1910," *Labor History* (Spring 1983), pp. 198-222.
28. Clarke J. Fitzpatrick and Elliott Buse, *Fifty Years of Suretyship and Insurance* (Baltimore, MD, 1946), pp. 20-21, 46-47.
29. Viviana A. Rotman Zelizer, *Morals and Markets: The Development of Life Insurance in the United States* (New York: Columbia University Press, 1979).
30. J. Owen Stalson, *Marketing Life Insurance: Its History in America* (Homewood, IL: Richard D. Irwin, Inc., 1969).
31. Shepard B. Clough, *A Century of American Life Insurance* (New York: Columbia University Press, 1946).
32. Zelizer, pp. 91-147.
33. Morton Keller, *The Life Insurance Enterprise, 1885-1910* (Cambridge, MA: Harvard University Press, 1963). Anita Rapone, *The Guardian Life Insurance Company, 1860-1920* (New York: New York University Press, 1987).
34. Thomas L. Wenck, "The Historical Development of Standard Policies," *The Journal of Risk and Insurance* (December 1968), pp. 537-550.
35. Delancey v. Rockingham Farmers Mutual Insurance Company 52 N.H. 581, 587 (1873).
36. Morton Keller, *Regulating a New Economy* (Cambridge, MA: Harvard University Press, 1990), pp. 23-30.
37. Russell B. Nye, *Midwestern Progressive Politics* (New York: Harper & Row, 1965), p. 60.
38. Nye, p. 61.
39. Munn v. Illinois 94 U.S. 113, 146 (1877).

40. Herbert Hovenkamp, *Enterprise and the American Law* (Cambridge, MA: Harvard University Press, 1991), pp. 128-130.

41. *Report on the Joint Committee of the Senate and Assembly of the State of New York Appointed to Investigate Corrupt Practices in Connection with Legislation, and the Affairs of Insurance Companies Other Than Those Doing Life Insurance Business* (Albany, NY, 1911), I, p. 65.

42. H. Roger Grant, *Insurance Reform: Consumer Action in the Progressive Era* (Ames, IA: The Iowa State University Press, 1979), p. 102.

43. German Alliance Insurance Company v. Lewis, U.S. Supreme Court (1914).

44. Grant, *Insurance Reform*, p. 107.

45. Maple Flooring Association v. United States, 268 U.S. 564, 45 S.Ct. 582 (1925).

46. Paul v. Virginia (1869), 8 Wall, pp. 183-184.

47. Charles D. Weller, "The McCarran-Ferguson Act's Antitrust Exemption for Insurance: Language, History and Policy," *Duke Law Journal* (1978), pp. 587-643.

48. National Association of Insurance Commissioners, All-Industry Rating Bills, June 12, 1946.

49. James F. Perry, "The McCarran-Ferguson Act: An Invitation to State Action," *CPCU Journal*, vol. 44 (September 1991), pp. 162-173.

50. William H. A. Carr, *Perils: Named and Unnamed* (New York: McGraw-Hill Book Company, 1967), p. 280.

51. *Proceedings of the National Convention of Insurance Commissioners* (1914), p. 4.

52. G. F. Michelbacher, *Multiple Line Insurance* (New York: McGraw-Hill Book Company, 1957), p. 4.

53. William D. Winter, "The Need for Research," Address to The Mariners Club in Philadelphia, May 3, 1954. *The Multiple Line Concept and the Need for Research* (New York: Atlantic Mutual Insurance Company, 1954), p. 56.

54. Winter, "Need for Research," p. 57.

55. Winter, *The Multiple Line Concept*, p. 34.

56. David Lynn Bickelhaupt, *Transition to Multiple-Line Insurance Companies* (Homewood, IL: Richard D. Irwin, Inc., 1961), p. 50.

57. *Sharing the Risk, How the Nation's Business, Homes and Autos Are Insured*, 3rd ed. (New York: Insurance Information Institute, 1989), pp. 145-146.

CHAPTER 2

Risk Management and Insurance

As the preceding chapter suggested, insurance has evolved into a major business by helping individuals, organizations, and society to manage risk. This chapter adds a formal dimension to that observation. Exposures to loss can best be analyzed and treated through a systematic risk management process. Such an analysis can lead to the selection of the most appropriate of a variety of risk management techniques. Insurance is one of those techniques.

Not all exposures to loss are well suited to insurance. This chapter explains the ideal characteristics of insurable loss exposures and describes the benefits and drawbacks inherent in insurance.

The final section of the chapter provides an overview of the coverages available through the more common types of property-liability insurance policies and describes the loss exposures addressed by each.

LOSS EXPOSURES

A *loss exposure* is any condition or situation that presents a possibility of financial loss, whether or not an actual loss ever occurs. Specific loss exposures will be examined later. For now a few examples of some of the exposures faced by an appliance manufacturer illustrate the basic concept.

1. *A factory building owned by the firm could be damaged or destroyed by a fire, a windstorm, an earthquake, or some other peril.* The business would have to do without the building and lose the income it generates or pay the cost to replace it. Even with replacement, the firm's income would diminish for a time.

2. *A visitor to the factory could be injured while on the premises.* The business might be held legally liable to pay damages to the guest.

3. *Solvents used in the manufacturing process could pollute the environment.* As a generator of pollutants, the manufacturer could be held legally liable for harm to the environment caused by its solvents and could also be ordered to pay substantial cleanup costs.

4. *Appliances manufactured by the firm could cause bodily injury to members of the public.* The manufacturer could be held legally liable to pay damages to injured consumers.

5. *While working in the factory, employees of the firm could be injured.* An employer is liable under workers compensation statutes for injured employees' lost wages as well as associated medical costs.

6. *If sales are low, the firm could lose its investment in a new product.* Of course, if sales are high, the firm could earn a very healthy profit. This possibility illustrates a so-called "business risk," in which some chance of loss is voluntarily assumed by a business in exchange for a probable gain.

Businesses are not the only organizations facing loss exposures. For example:

- A person who owns a house is subject to a possible loss of that property as the result of a fire, a windstorm, or an earthquake.
- If the family breadwinner becomes disabled, dependent family members could lose their means of support.
- Governmental entities such as municipalities, as well as other nonprofit organizations, can be held legally liable to others for bodily injury and property damage. For example, a pedestrian could trip and fall on a government-owned sidewalk or in a hospital corridor and seek to recover damages.

All of these are loss *exposures.* Whether or not a loss of a certain type has ever occurred in the past, the possibility of a future loss can be recognized. Even if no actual loss ever does occur, that does not detract from the importance of loss exposures: They represent a *possibility* of financial loss.

Two significant types of exposures—those that often can be treated with property and liability insurance—are property loss exposures and liability loss exposures.

Property Loss Exposures

Property loss exposures exist because some party depends on property to accomplish certain objectives. The property has usefulness which, in turn, gives the property economic value. This value can decline or be lost. A property loss exposure has three elements:

1. *Property*—the item(s) of property subject to loss, damage, or destruction
2. *Perils*—the causes that might lead to loss, damage, or destruction of property
3. *Loss Consequences*—the financial result when a peril causes property to be lost, damaged, or destroyed

Item(s) of Property Subject to Loss. Property exposed to loss can be classified as real property (that is, real estate) or personal property.

- *Real property* includes land, as well as buildings and structures attached to the land. A house, a fence, a swimming pool, a concrete driveway, and an underground sewer pipe are all items of real property, as is the land where they are situated.
- *Personal property* includes all other types of tangible or intangible property, such as inventory, equipment, fixtures, supplies, machinery, computers, money, securities, books, animals, autos, patents, and copyrights. (The term "personal," in the language of insurance, often refers to individuals and families. However, "personal property" may be owned by any party—individuals, families, businesses, or other organizations.)

Perils, or Causes of Loss. A *peril* is a cause of loss, damage, or destruction. Many insurance policies use the everyday phrase "cause of loss," while others use the more technical word "peril." "Peril" and "cause of loss" mean essentially the same thing, and the terms often are used interchangeably.

Most perils cause loss to property by leaving it in an altered, less functional state. A fire may change a wooden building to a pile of ashes. Smoke may change attractive draperies to sooty, smelly pieces of cloth.

Some perils do not alter the state of property, but they nevertheless cause loss by affecting the owner's ability to possess or use the property. Theft often has this effect. A stolen camera may be unaltered, and it may remain usable. However, it is not usable by its rightful owner, who has suffered a loss as surely as if the camera had been flattened by a steamroller.

Loss Consequences. A variety of consequences may result when property is lost, damaged, or destroyed by a peril. Some are immediately obvious and readily measurable. Others involve a certain "time element" and have an impact only as time elapses following the immediate event. Among the potential consequences of loss of, damage to, or destruction of property are the following:

- *Reduction in value.* When a peril damages or destroys a building, an auto, a jacket, or other property, the property usually is reduced in value. Many losses involve only a partial reduction in value. Property that is completely destroyed is reduced in value to zero, at least to the owner or user of the property. Often, however, some salvageable items can be sold to others. (What we have called "reduction in value" often is referred to as "direct loss." We prefer to avoid that terminology because of widespread inconsistencies in defining the antonym, "indirect loss.")

- *Cost of debris removal.* Before an item of property can be restored, the debris of damaged property often must be removed. In some cases, such as a fire-damaged high-rise building, for example, these costs can be substantial indeed. In contrast, the cost of towing a damaged auto from an accident scene usually is modest.

- *Extra cost to replace.* Following a loss, the costs of repair or of replacement property often exceed the amount by which the original property was reduced in value by the loss. For example, a contractor may charge $100,000 (the "replacement cost") to construct a new dwelling to replace one that before the loss had a depreciated "actual cash value" of $80,000.

- *Loss of income.* When income-producing property is damaged, destroyed, or lost, the owner may receive no income—or a reduced income—for a period lasting until the property is restored, and perhaps longer. For example, following damage by fire, a retail store may produce no income until the building is repaired and the shelves are restored and restocked with undamaged merchandise. Even then, the store's sales volume may not return immediately to what it would have been had there been no fire. (Because the type of insurance that provides reimbursement for such loss of income was formerly called "business interruption" insurance, insurance practitioners sometimes apply the label "business interruption" to this loss consequence. The term "business income" also is used, reflecting the names of contemporary policies covering this exposure.)

- *Extra expenses.* When property is damaged, destroyed, or lost, some organizations may avoid an interruption in operations by spending extra money. An attorney, for example, might rent another office on a short-term basis while damage to her own office is being repaired. Similarly, a family whose house has been damaged might incur extra expenses ("additional living expenses") to rent temporary quarters while the damage is repaired. Another example involves the cost of renting a substitute auto to temporarily replace one that has been stolen, until a permanent replacement can be purchased.

This is only a partial list of the types of consequences that may be a part of property losses.

Any or all of these consequences may be irreversibly incurred as a result of a single event in which property is damaged by a peril. The extent of some consequences, however, depends not so much on the amount of damage to property as on the degree to which the ability to use the property is diminished and the time that will elapse before the property can be restored. Loss of income, and extra expenses to operate, therefore, are said to involve a "time element."

Property Loss Terminology in Practice. An actual *loss* occurs when a peril causes property to be lost, damaged, or destroyed with adverse financial consequences. The possibility that the event could occur is a *loss exposure*. The event itself, involving property, peril, and consequence(s), is called a *loss* or, more completely, a *property loss*.

A property loss may also be referred to by different labels, depending on whether emphasis is being placed on the property, the peril, or the consequences.

- When focusing on the type of property, insurance practitioners often refer to a "building loss" or a "personal property loss," regardless of the peril involved.
- When emphasis is on perils (causes of loss), one might refer to a "fire loss," a "smoke loss," or a "theft loss."
- When focusing on loss consequences, insurance practitioners may refer to a "business income loss," an "extra expense loss," or an "additional living expense loss," regardless of the type of property or peril involved.

In other situations, insurance practitioners may label a loss by referring to the policy providing coverage. Fire damage to a house might be referred to as a "homeowners loss," while concurrent damage to a car in the attached garage might be referred to as an "auto loss."

In practice, these same labels are loosely applied to exposures. One might refer to a building exposure, a fire exposure, a business interruption exposure, or a homeowners exposure.

Liability Loss Exposures

In short, a liability loss exposure involves the possibility that a claim for damages will be brought by some outside party. A *liability loss exposure* is a set of circumstances that presents the possibility that one must spend time and money for the investigation, negotiation, settlement, defense, and/or payment of a claim or suit that arises out of a real or alleged failure to fulfill an obligation or duty imposed by law.

This definition of liability loss exposures focuses on the possibility of a *claim* for damages, rather than on the potential *payment* of damages. Many liability claims are groundless or involve situations in which the defendant ultimately is not held responsible for paying damages. They nevertheless are liability "losses" because of the time and expense involved in resolving them. Every claim requires a response, and many can be closed or settled only after substantial legal expenses have been incurred. Where a formal lawsuit is involved, failure to acknowledge the suit and offer a defense as appropriate may lead to a default judgment. Therefore, even groundless, frivolous, and fraudulent claims and suits require attention.

Liability claims may be based on an obligation or duty imposed by common law, statutes, or contract law.

Common Law. The common law is a body of legally enforceable principles and rules of conduct that derive their authority mainly from custom and legal precedent, including previous court rulings involving similar circumstances. Court decisions, commonly cited in a format like "So-and-so v. Such-and-such," are decisions that become part of the common law.

Statutes. Statutes are written enactments of legislative bodies (state, federal, local "laws") that alter or amend the common law, formalize or codify the common law, create liabilities that never existed at common law, or eliminate those that did. For example, workers compensation statutes create liabilities by making the employer financially responsible for virtually all on-the-job employee injuries, without regard to the employer's fault or lack of fault in causing the injury.

Contracts. Contracts are legally enforceable agreements that spell out the promises and responsibilities of the parties involved. For example, a lease agreement on a commercial building may specify that the tenant assumes responsibility for all injuries occurring on the premises.

Liability Loss Terminology in Practice. Insurance and risk management practitioners loosely refer to specific types of liability losses in many ways, often labeling them according to the type of insurance that might cover the exposure. For example, a claim for damages arising out of a product defect might be referred to as a "products liability loss," and the possibility of such a claim might be referred to as a "products liability exposure." Likewise, the possibility of professional liability claims against a physician might be referred to as a "professional liability exposure" or a "malpractice exposure." Losses arising out of an employer's liability under workers compensation statutes might be referred to as "workers compensation losses."

Property and Liability Exposures Compared

Property loss exposures tend to differ from liability loss exposures with regard to the measurability of the exposure and the incidence in time of the financial consequences involved. These characteristics often affect the ways in which the exposures are treated. Although the characteristics below apply as generalizations, there clearly are specific situations in which they are not applicable.

Measurability. The maximum extent of property loss exposures depends to a high degree on loss consequences that may be evaluated with some effort in advance of any loss. For example:

● The reduction in value of property cannot exceed the pre-loss value of that property.
● The loss of income that might follow property damage is directly related to the amount of income normally generated by undamaged property.

In short, the value of the property, the future level of income generated, and other related factors create a natural limitation on the amount that might be lost if the property is damaged or destroyed.

Some liability loss exposures, such as those involving a party's possible liability for damage to a particular item of property, are limited in the same ways as property loss exposures. However, because there are no natural limitations and usually no direct relationship to values involved in most cases, it is much more difficult, if not impossible, to predict confidently the potential amount of a liability loss. Moreover, substantial claims can result from the failure of an item with relatively little intrinsic value—a few defective rivets could conceivably lead to an airplane crash. Chance circumstances may lead a runaway truck to collide with a school bus full of children, rather than a garbage truck full of trash. And jury awards are unpredictable at best.

Timing of Loss Payments. In most situations, property losses are resolved within a relatively short period of time, generally limited by the amount of time it takes to repair the damage or acquire replacement property. Liability claims, in contrast, can drag out for many years. There sometimes is a period during which the claimant is unaware of the injury or damage. Delays in negotiation and navigating the legal system may consume several years after a claim is made. Even after a claim is settled, cash payments to the claimant may actually take place over a long period of time. For example, a claimant who is permanently disabled as the result of an industrial accident may receive disability income payments for ten or twenty years or longer.

THE RISK MANAGEMENT PROCESS

Risk management has been defined as the organized treatment of loss exposures. With various degrees of formality, the risk management function is performed by virtually every individual, family, business, or organization.

- Many individuals or families deal with their loss exposures in a very informal way by "trying to be safe" and buying the insurance coverages that may be mandated by law, required by a lender, or recommended by an insurance representative. Others, generally those with more assets, take a more formal or structured approach as part of a personal financial planning program. Within a family, the risk management function generally is performed by the person(s) who assume(s) responsibility for financial matters.
- Small or medium-sized businesses or organizations differ widely in their approach to risk management. Small businesses tend to use a family-like approach to risk management matters, often relying primarily on the expertise of an insurance agent or broker. Medium-sized businesses may assign part-time "risk management" responsibilities to a treasurer, accountant, or personnel manager—who may rely on the expertise of an insurance agent or broker or, for more complex matters, retain an outside risk management consultant.
- Large businesses and organizations, especially those with major loss exposures (such as a large hospital, which faces the potential of substantial malpractice claims) often have a full-time risk manager or risk management department.

The risk management function is performed by applying a systematic process. The *risk management process* can be defined as *the process for making and carrying out decisions that will minimize the adverse effects of accidental loss.*

The risk management process involves five steps:

1. Identifying and analyzing loss exposures
2. Examining the feasibility of alternative risk management techniques
3. Selecting the best risk management technique(s)
4. Implementing the techniques
5. Monitoring the program

In principle, these steps are taken one at a time in the above sequence. However, the experienced risk management professional recognizes the relationships among these various steps. For example, as each loss exposure is identified, the experienced risk management professional simultaneously begins considering alternative ways of dealing with that exposure. Many exposures are fairly routine and can be handled in routine ways, while others require creativity.

Identifying and Analyzing Loss Exposures

Except by chance, it is impossible to manage loss exposures that have not been recognized. The risk management process therefore begins with identifying loss exposures and analyzing their potential impact.

Identifying Loss Exposures. Exposure identification is challenging because exposures are easily overlooked. Moreover, loss exposures are subject to frequent change. An approach to effective exposure identification should be both systematic and continuous.

Airplane pilots walk around their airplanes and look for possible problems before departure. "Looking at" the airplane is useful, but relatively unsystematic. Therefore, even the most experienced pilots also work step-by-step through a formal checklist to ensure that they have not failed to examine a single item that could be critical to safety. "Looking around" is important in understanding loss exposures, but a systematic approach also is necessary.

Several systematic exposure identification approaches have been developed, including the following:

- *Checklist or questionnaire approach.* A checklist is a prepared form listing many of the loss exposures faced by various entities, which can simply be checked "yes" or "no." A similar approach involves the use of a fill-in-the-blanks questionnaire that may allow for descriptive information, amounts, or values. Such checklists are published by insurers, the American Management Association, the Risk and Insurance Management Society (RIMS), the International Risk Management Institute, and others. Some organizations or associations have developed specialized checklists or questionnaires for their own use.

    Many published checklists are limited to loss exposures that can be insured, and they overlook other important exposures that also require treatment. If any are so thorough that they list all conceivable exposures, they probably are also so long as to be unmanageable.

The value of a questionnaire varies in direct proportion to the skill of the user. An experienced insurance and risk management professional understands the implications of various items on the checklist and uses the checklist to trigger additional questions or ideas.

- *Financial statement approach.* This approach has special appeal to people with an accounting or finance perspective, because it begins with the analysis of an organization's financial statements (such as the balance sheet, income statement, and budget and supporting documents). Each item in the financial statements is analyzed to determine the loss exposures it reflects. For example, an entry for "finished goods inventory" in the balance sheet of a manufacturing firm indicates a property loss exposure and gives some indication of its magnitude. This entry might also lead to related questions such as the damageability of these items, where they are kept, how they are transported, and any related environmental hazards.

- *Flowchart approach.* Flowchart diagrams, often containing labeled blocks connected by arrows, show the relationships of various operations. A flowchart can help to illustrate what an organization does, the sequence in which activities take place, and the nature and use of the resources involved.

  For example, a manufacturer's flowchart may start with the acquisition of raw materials and end with the delivery of the finished product to the ultimate consumer. Individual entries on the flowchart, the processes involved, and the means by which products move from one process to the next can be used to trigger further inquiry that helps identify and understand loss exposures.

  Flowcharts can be particularly useful in identifying critical exposures. For example, a flowchart may clearly demonstrate that every item produced by a certain manufacturer must go through the spray painting booth at some point in the manufacturing process. Knowing the fire hazards involved in spray painting, the experienced analyst might recognize that this booth presents a critical property loss exposure. An explosion at this single location might tie up the entire production line. Spray painting operations also can present liability exposures involving environmental hazards.

- *Loss analysis.* It is desirable to examine loss records to identify the exposures that have revealed themselves through losses and to determine what hazards may have contributed to the loss. However, loss analysis helps to identify only loss exposures that have already led to an actual loss, many of which may already have been treated. Loss analysis alone may not reveal exposures that have not yet resulted in a mishap.

Whenever possible, it is highly desirable to supplement other methods of identifying loss exposures with a *personal inspection* or on-site visit. There is no substitute for "being there" to get a taste for loss exposures. Moreover, personal inspections often reveal hazards that do not show up on paper. For example, one might notice auto seat belts stuffed under the seat cushion and obviously not being used. Or one might notice drill press operators with long hair dangling dangerously while they work—an accidental "scalping" waiting to happen.

Checklists, financial statements, flowchart analyses, and personal inspections can be supplemented with other approaches for identifying loss exposures, some of which are examined in other CPCU courses.

Measuring Potential Frequency and Severity. *Identification* implies recognizing all loss exposures that could possibly result in a loss. Obviously, some exposures are more significant than others. The relative significance of the various exposures is determined by measuring the frequency ("how often?") and severity ("how costly?") of losses resulting from that exposure:

- By multiplying expected annual frequency times expected loss severity, one can calculate the expected total dollar losses for a loss exposure for a typical year.
- By evaluating maximum annual loss frequency and maximum loss severity, one can assess the potential for losses of disastrous proportions from a given exposure.
- By assessing the variation in annual loss frequency, individual loss severity, and total annual dollar losses, one can decide how much confidence can reasonably be placed in these evaluations.

As mentioned earlier, past experience is not necessarily a good indicator of what will happen in the future, but it is a starting point. (The phrase "past experience" is admittedly redundant, as there really is no other kind of experience. However, it is deeply embedded in insurance jargon, and we will continue to use this phrase as it is used by insurance and risk management practitioners—who might even occasionally use the oxymoron "future experience.") Analysis of potential frequency and severity should be based not only on historical (past) losses, but also on the characteristics of current loss exposures and any changes in the exposures over time. In general, the larger the number of exposure units for a given exposure, the more credible are the predictions generated from past loss data. Frequency and severity predictions help to prioritize the exposures that need treatment so that risk management resources can be devoted to the exposures for which they are most needed.

Examining the Feasibility of Alternative Risk Management Techniques. Risk management techniques seek to eliminate loss exposures, to control loss exposures that are not eliminated, and to finance (pay for) losses that occur despite the controls.

Exposure Avoidance. The risk management technique known as "exposure avoidance" is used when a party decides not to incur a loss exposure or to eliminate one that already exists. Many medical students, for example, choose not to become obstetricians because obstetricians often are targets of large professional liability (malpractice) claims. And the manufacturers of hand-held hair dryers discontinued the practice of using asbestos insulation in their dryers once the cancer-causing properties of asbestos were known.

By definition, exposure avoidance reduces to zero the probability of loss from the avoided exposure. If this objective has not been accomplished, the exposure has not been avoided. Often, discontinuing an existing activity avoids losses from future activities, but it does not eliminate outstanding exposures that may still arise from past activities. For example, a sporting goods manufacturer may quit making football helmets because of claims for injuries connected with their use. Product liability loss exposures arising out of future helmet sales have been avoided, but claims could still arise from the helmets already in use.

Loss Prevention. The risk management technique of loss prevention seeks to lower the probable frequency of loss from a given exposure or set of exposures. For example, the use of pressure relief valves on a boiler is intended to prevent explosions by keeping the pressure in the boiler from exceeding a certain level.

Loss Reduction. The loss reduction technique aims to lower the severity of losses that occur. Automatic sprinkler systems are a classic application of this technique. Sprinklers do not keep a fire from starting, but they are intended to limit or extinguish fires that have already created enough heat to activate the sprinkler head.

Many measures apply both the loss prevention and the loss reduction techniques; they serve to prevent some losses and to reduce others. Burglar alarm systems, for example, may prevent losses to the extent that they keep burglars from trying. However, burglar alarms generally are not activated until a burglar begins to enter the premises. Their primary function, therefore, is to cause burglars to be caught or to limit the amount of time available to burglars who are not apprehended.

Separation of Loss Exposures. The separation technique involves arranging an organization's activities and resources so as to minimize the impact of a single event. For example, instead of placing all inventory in a single warehouse, subject to damage by a single disaster, a business might use several smaller warehouses.

Duplication. The duplication technique essentially relies on back-ups or spares—copies of critical records, items, sources, or capabilities. Computer tapes, copies of accounts receivable, duplicate manuscripts, and the like often can be inexpensively made and stored in a remote, protected location. Critical repair parts or duplicate machines can be kept on hand for immediate replacement. An electric generating plant, for example, may keep one functioning generator off-line and ready for immediate use if another generator should fail, so that power can be provided virtually without interruption. Increasingly important, for many organizations, is an arrangement to provide backup data processing capacity should the organization's own computer facility be damaged.

Noninsurance Contracts. Nearly every adult person and nearly every business enters into a variety of contractual agreements through which loss exposures are shifted from one party to another. Examples include auto rental agreements, apartment lease agreements, purchase orders, credit card agreements, and construction contracts. In some cases, the entire exposure is transferred to another party; in other cases, only the financial consequences of a loss are transferred.

Insurance. Although insurance is "only" one of several broad techniques used in risk management, it almost always is an important component of a risk management program for even the wealthiest organizations. From a risk management viewpoint, insurance is a formal device through which the potential financial consequences of certain specified loss exposures are transferred to an insurance company. Specific coverages and policies are discussed later in this chapter.

Retention. Retention is, simply, retaining (keeping) the financial consequences of a loss exposure. The financial consequences of any exposure that has not been avoided, and that has not been transferred through insurance or a noninsurance contract, are invariably retained.

Retention may be intentional or unintentional. After thoroughly analyzing the alternatives, it often is apparent that retention is the best means of handling the financial consequences of a given exposure, perhaps because no insurance or noninsurance transfer is available. Unintentional retention may result from inadequate exposure identification and analysis, or from an incomplete evaluation of alternatives.

Retention may be partial or total. Partial retention is involved when insurance is purchased with a deductible. With auto physical damage insurance, for example, a policyholder may agree to pay by himself (that is, to retain) the first $500 of any collision damage, while the insurance company agrees to pay damage amounts beyond $500.

Selecting the Best Risk Management Technique(s)

After considering how various risk management techniques might be applied to particular loss exposures, the next step is to establish and apply criteria to determine, for a particular organization, what combination of risk management techniques is "best" in serving that organization's objectives. Some loss exposures are treated with a single risk management technique. However, risk management techniques usually are used in combination.

- As mentioned above, insurance with a deductible involves a mixture of the retention and insurance techniques. (In recognition of their reduced exposure, insurers usually reduce premiums as deductible amounts are increased.)
- Motorists who purchase cars with airbags (an application of the loss reduction technique) generally also purchase insurance protecting themselves against medical expenses arising from auto accidents. (Premium discounts may be available.)
- When accounts receivable records are insured, the insurer may require that duplicate records be kept at another location (an application of the duplication technique) or may provide a premium discount when duplicate records exist.

For most loss exposures, the synergistic effect of combining risk management techniques certainly should be considered. Usually it is appropriate to consider controls that may prevent or reduce losses, as well as measures for financing those losses that occur despite the controls.

Cost/Benefit Analysis. To make a thorough analysis leading to a defensible risk management decision, three forecasts are required:

1. A projection of the frequency and severity of expected losses
2. For each feasible combination of risk management measures, a forecast of their expected effect on the frequency, severity, and predictability of these projected losses
3. A projection of the cost involved in applying the various measures (for example, the cost of insurance premiums or loss prevention devices)

Based on the above forecasts, an entity can perform a cost/benefit analysis in order to identify the risk management technique or combination of techniques that will treat its loss exposures at the lowest bottom-line cost, taking tax considerations into account. In practice, it often is difficult to develop meaningful data.

Nonfinancial Considerations. Dollar costs and benefits usually are not the only criteria that should be considered in arriving at a risk management decision. An organization or family also may place a great deal of value on criteria such as maintaining stable earnings, keeping the business in operation, or getting a "quiet night's sleep." As a result of such considerations, an organization may choose the technique or combination of techniques that does not have the lowest dollar cost.

Ethical Implications. Often the risk management decision that produces the best financial result, at least in the short run, is unacceptable for ethical reasons and must therefore be rejected. Although it is easy to recognize the ethical constraints involved in many risk management decisions, it is not always as easy to determine the most ethical course of action. In Johnson Controls' battery manufacturing operation, the environment contained high concentrations of ambient lead. Eight employees became pregnant while maintaining blood lead levels exceeding that noted by OSHA as critical for a worker planning to have a family. In response, Johnson decided to establish a policy barring women, except those whose infertility was medically documented, from jobs involving actual or potential lead exposure exceeding the OSHA standard.[1] This decision may not have been entirely altruistic or nonfinancial in nature—it also tended to prevent future claims by these women or their children. Was it an ethical decision? Perhaps. But the court ruled that it constituted illegal sexual discrimination against the women who wanted these jobs. We did not mention the Johnson case to take sides in a complex issue, but to provide an example of the ethical difficulties involved in making some risk management decisions. Other difficult ethical decisions may involve the level of pollutants that may be discharged, the satisfactory disposition of unavoidable toxic wastes, and the extent of quality control applied to consumer products.

Minimum Expected Cost Method. One approach to decisions involving both financial and nonfinancial considerations is the minimum expected cost method. This method involves assigning a specific dollar worth to those "values" that usually are not measured in monetary terms. This dollar worth may be derived implicitly and informally in evaluating the costs of various measures.

For many organizations, for example, a lapse of computer services would interrupt many important operations. Numerous firms sell standby backup computer services in various forms (an example of the duplication technique). These services can be expensive. Suppose backup computer service can be made available to an organization on a standby basis for $100,000 per year, with additional fees if the service actually is used. The benefits of remaining in operation may not be measurable in purely financial terms, but the decision must be made whether it is "worth" $100,000 per year to utilize this application of the duplication technique in order to prevent computer-related lapses.

Implementing the Decision

After making a decision regarding the risk management technique(s) to be used, the next step is to implement the decision. Implementation requires action and further decisions. It may be necessary to purchase loss reduction devices or to contract for loss prevention services. Contracts must be written or revised. Insurance policies must be requested and paid for. Retention programs may have to be funded.

Many implementation-related details will already have been identified in the process of identifying and evaluating alternatives. Remaining details, such as the exact placement of fire extinguishers, the negotiation of contract revisions, the timing of insurance premium payments, or the actual deposit of funds to pay claims under a funded retention program, need to be addressed in implementing the decision.

Monitoring the Program

A risk management program must be monitored to determine whether and when it should be modified. Ongoing experience with the program may suggest that the best technique or combination of techniques was not selected originally or that the choices made were not properly implemented. Conditions also may change so much that, although the original decision and implementation were correct, a different solution is more appropriate at a later time.

To monitor a program, one must establish performance standards, check adherence to these standards, and decide what degree of noncompliance calls for a correction. If a correction is in order, one should repeat the risk management process.

Although every risk management program should be informally monitored on a continuous basis, it is desirable to schedule a thorough periodic review. For example, the program might be reviewed annually as insurance policies come up for renewal (a convenient time to review exposures and costs). A more thorough review might be done, say, every three or five years—including, perhaps, soliciting alternative insurance proposals from other insurers.

INSURANCE AS A RISK MANAGEMENT TECHNIQUE

Although there are many formal techniques available to treat loss exposures, the most widely used may be insurance. Insurance entails a transfer of the financial consequences of loss exposures from the insured to the insurer in exchange for the payment of a premium. The organizational form of insurance enterprises varies significantly, but whether insurance is provided by stock companies, mutual companies, lloyds organizations, reciprocal insurers, or even some form of captive insurer, the insurance technique has some important common elements.

Some loss exposures are too trivial to justify explicit, formal insurance arrangements. Other loss exposures are so monumental or unpredictable that no one would be willing to accept the transfer of such risk. For exposures with the right characteristics, however, the insurance device provides an excellent risk management technique. In addition to effecting the transfer of the financial consequences of loss exposures, insurance offers a number of related benefits, although it also has certain drawbacks.

Ideal Characteristics of an Insurable Exposure

Private insurance companies are able and willing to insure some loss exposures but not others. Therefore, it is helpful to consider the ideal characteristics of those property and liability loss exposures that are considered commercially insurable. Those that do not come close enough to these ideal characteristics are not suitable for insurance by a private insurance company, although some form of government insurance program may be available.

A commercially insurable exposure ideally possesses the following characteristics:

- The exposure involves pure risk rather than speculative risk.
- Uncertainty exists as to time or probability of loss.
- The happening, time, and amount of an insured loss can clearly be determined.
- A large number of exposures are insured.
- A loss will not simultaneously affect many insureds.
- Insurance is economically feasible.

It must be emphasized that these are *ideal characteristics*. Every type of insurance covers some exposures that do not *completely* meet *all* of these criteria. Some exposures come close to the ideal and are insurable, while others present problems so substantial as to make them uninsurable.

Pure Risk. While the term "risk" is difficult to define satisfactorily, it may generally be characterized as "uncertainty regarding loss." For purposes of insurance and risk management, risk often is subdivided into two categories: pure risk and speculative risk.

- A *pure risk* presents only two possible outcomes: financial loss or no financial loss. The possibilities are either undesirable (loss) or neutral (no loss), but in no case beneficial. A pure risk presents no opportunity for a gain. The uncertainty whether a person's auto could be damaged in a collision involves a pure risk, because the best possible outcome is that no collision occurs.

- A *speculative risk* presents a situation with three possible outcomes. Added to the two presented by pure risk is the third possible outcome—the possibility of financial gain. An investor who purchases shares of stock hopes that the stock will gain in value, but the value of the stock also could decrease in value or remain unchanged.

With rare exceptions, insurance has been applied to pure risks but not to speculative risks. Many speculative risks fail to possess the characteristics of an insurable exposure, which are detailed below. For others, there simply is no sound reason to consider the use of insurance. Among other things, people assume speculative risks in the hope of financial gain, and the premium that would necessarily be charged for insurance would tend to neutralize not only potential losses, but also potential gains.

In the context of commercial property and liability insurance, the speculative risks that tend to be unsuitable for insurance sometimes are referred to as *business risks.* For example, suppose Steve and Sue open a restaurant that they naturally expect to be a successful business. Of course, the possibility also exists that the business will be unsuccessful. They assume this speculative risk voluntarily, and the extent to which the restaurant will succeed is largely the product of their planning and management.

Also, many manufacturers face the possibility that a product will not deliver its expected standard of performance. Failure to perform, in some broad sense, is the result of an error or oversight in product design, testing, or advertising, and it generally is not insurable.

Uncertainty as to Probability or Time of Loss. When there is no uncertainty regarding loss, there is no risk, and insurance would serve no purpose. Uncertainty is absent when a loss cannot possibly happen. By definition, an exposure that is avoided cannot possibly lead to a loss, and there is no loss exposure to transfer to an insurer.

Uncertainty also is absent when the insured has complete control over the happening or nonhappening of a covered loss. There is a chance of loss, but the *insured* faces no uncertainty. It would be unwise for an insurer knowingly to provide insurance against losses that can be caused at will by the party who, in turn, will receive payment from the insurer. Otherwise, an insured who owns a building that is no longer needed could simply burn it down and turn in a fire insurance claim. Insurance policies normally exclude coverage for losses that are expected or intended from the standpoint of the insured. In addition, insurers' underwriting practices are intended to preclude insurance in situations where a serious moral hazard exists—such as fire insurance on a vacant, obsolete building that has no economic value.

Between the losses that cannot happen and the losses that are certain to happen lies a vast middle ground of losses involving uncertainty as to the probability of loss or the timing of the loss.

Probability of Loss. From the viewpoint of the insurance buyer, the main reason for purchasing insurance usually is the uncertainty of whether, or how often, a particular type of loss will occur. Insurance companies handle this uncertainty by pooling the exposures of many different insureds. Although losses are uncertain from the viewpoint of the insurance buyer, from the viewpoint of the insurer, it is desirable that the losses of a large number of insureds be somewhat calculable and predictable. Otherwise, it would be impossible to determine an appropriate premium to charge.

Some liability exposures are difficult or impossible to insure because loss frequency and severity cannot satisfactorily be predicted. Changing legal standards and increasingly large jury awards have, at times, made insurers reluctant to provide certain types of liability coverage such as products liability insurance or medical professional liability insurance. The huge costs of pollution cleanups combined with severe and changing legal standards of liability have tended to make pollution liability nearly uninsurable in recent years.

Time of Loss. Generally speaking, insurance deals with uncertainty regarding the probability of loss. However, in some cases the risk involves not whether a loss will occur, but when. There is no question regarding the frequency or severity relating to the exposures covered by life insurance. Every person dies, and the death occurs one time. Yet, life insurance not only exists but is one of the oldest, most successful forms of commercial insurance. The risk associated with life insurance is not *whether* the insured will die, but *when*.

In at least one unusual liability case, the timing risk was virtually the only uncertainty that was insured with a controversial coverage known as "retroactive insurance" following the MGM Grand Hotel fire in which a number of people were killed or injured. The insured event had already taken place, and the number of claims could be estimated with reasonable accuracy. However, these claims would be paid over an indeterminate period of years as a number of lawsuits were handled. In this case, the hotel was able to purchase "retroactive liability insurance" with a single premium, transferring to an insurance company the risks associated with the timing of actual claims payments. The insurance company could earn investment income on the money it held until claims were actually paid. A not-incidental benefit to the hotel was its ability to take the premium cost as a tax deduction which otherwise would have to be spread over a number of years as claims were paid.

Definite Happening, Time, and Amount. Ideally, it should be obvious whether an insured event has occurred, and insurers attempt to draft insurance policies that leave little doubt as to what events are covered. Insurance is best suited for covering potential losses that can later be determined to have happened at a specific time. Insurance policies typically provide coverage for a specific policy period, and the insurer is not obligated to pay for losses taking place outside that time period.

In practice, "definite time" does not often present a problem with property insurance since most losses involve a dramatic event that is immediately apparent. Even so, questions sometimes do develop for property losses resulting from employee theft, gradual contamination or pollution, or other perils that occur over a period of time. In liability insurance, questions often develop regarding the timing of the event that triggers coverage.

It would be difficult for insurance to function unless some method is established, before any loss occurs, to determine how much the insurer would pay if there is a loss. Insurance policies include many provisions intended to address this specific need.

Large Number of Insured Exposures. Insurance companies operate by pooling a number of exposures that otherwise would be borne by the insured individuals or organizations. If only a few exposures were covered, the insurer would face virtually the same uncertainties as the insured, and there would be no value in the insurance mechanism.

An ideally insurable exposure involves many nearly similar (homogeneous) exposure units, each of which has essentially the same loss exposures. Loss statistics can be maintained over time, and losses for the group as a whole can be predicted with a high degree of accuracy. The cost of these losses can then be spread among all members of the insured group.

In practice, few exposure units are completely identical, but those with similar characteristics can be treated as a group and the losses to the group can be analyzed, predicted, and insured. Personal auto insurance typically is handled by classifying each policyholder into a group that also includes a large number of other drivers with similar characteristics.

Even with auto insurance, few insurance companies insure such a large number of exposure units that their past loss experience is entirely reliable as a predictor of future losses. Statistical organizations accumulate information on the losses experienced by many different insurance companies and use this information to predict expected loss costs for an insured that falls into a particular category. Because of this pooled information, an insurance company might be able to insure only one policyholder in a particular category, basing the premium charge on the shared experience of other insurers. Pooling information is much more efficient than the alternative of setting a higher premium to compensate for the uncertainty of insuring unusual loss exposures.

Loss Not Simultaneously Affecting Many Insureds. Insurance is based on the premise that many insureds will pay premiums, but only a few will have losses. Insurance is not well suited for losses that are likely to affect many insureds at the same time. Losses resulting from war or a nuclear accident are excluded from almost all insurance policies for this reason. Other examples include catastrophic loss by flood or earthquake.

Unemployment is another example of an exposure that is not well suited to treatment by private insurance. While involuntary unemployment—the threat of being laid off—is a pure risk faced by large numbers of people, and the exposure might be definite in time and amount, unemployment often occurs as a result of a widespread economic downturn affecting many businesses. Unemployment insurance is, however, provided by government agencies, which are in a position to manage the exposure as a social program.

Another example is the risk that individual bank depositors could lose money in their bank accounts because of a bank insolvency. This exposure is insured—not by private insurers, but through a federal program that had to raise huge sums of money to cover losses in the early 1990s when economic conditions adversely affected many different banks across the country.

Insurers prevent the possibility of many losses from a single occurrence in several ways. They limit the amount of property insurance provided at a single location or within a limited geographic area, and they purchase reinsurance to protect against large losses. Large multi-line insurance companies also achieve a spread of risk by writing many different lines of insurance on individuals and businesses facing differing exposures. Even if one group of insureds—for example, those that manufactured a product using asbestos—sustain large unforeseen losses, losses are partially offset by premiums collected from insureds in other classes.

Economic Feasibility. Insurance companies tend to provide insurance, and insurance consumers tend to purchase insurance, only when it makes good economic sense. Exposures involving high loss frequency or low loss severity often fail to meet this criterion.

High-frequency losses often are predictable enough to be treated as current expenses or funded with a planned retention program that does not involve the overhead expenses of insurance. An example might be a shipper who ships a large number of low-value packages. Low-frequency losses, on the other hand, are characterized by the type of unpredictability that often lends itself to insurance treatment. An example would be fire damage to one's house.

While insurance works well for many low-frequency loss exposures, insurance may not be economically feasible for losses with a *very* low frequency, because there is no demand for protection against something that is highly unlikely (or is considered unlikely). Until Mt. Saint Helens erupted, most people thought the possibility of a volcanic eruption was practically nonexistent in the continental United States. Many property insurance policies made no specific reference to damage originating from volcanoes, and there was no demand for insurance against volcanic eruption. Likewise, people in many areas of the United States where earthquakes are possible but unlikely do not purchase earthquake insurance.

Most low-severity losses do not produce financial consequences so substantial that they cannot readily be managed with one's own resources. The consequences of spilling gravy onto a tie are a dry cleaning bill or, at worst, the cost of a new tie. The financial consequences of spilling a can of paint onto the shingled roof of a house would be much more severe.

Loss exposures involving *very* high severity and *very* low frequency, on the other hand, do not tend to be sound subjects for insurance by private insurance companies. An example might be the possibility of liability for radioactive contamination resulting from a problem with a nuclear power plant. Although loss frequency has been extremely low, the potential severity of contamination losses is so high that the resources of the entire worldwide insurance industry might be inadequate to pay the damages that might result from a single incident. The exposure is, however, insured through a complex mechanism that draws on worldwide insurance resources combined with statutory limits on an organization's maximum liability in a nuclear disaster.

Benefits of Insurance

The fundamental benefit of insurance, to the insurance buyer, is the insurer's promise to pay claims. In addition, insurers offer several related services, and insurance buyers receive several additional benefits.

Payment of Claims. In exchange for the insured's payment of a specified premium, the insurer agrees to protect the insured against specified types of potential losses. This agreement is stated in a legally enforceable contract, the insurance policy, in which the insurer agrees to make payments to or on behalf of the insured in the event of a covered loss. With liability insurance, the insurer also agrees to pay defense costs.

Related Services and Benefits. In addition to paying claims, insurers provide a number of related services. For some insurance buyers, some of these services may be more important than the actual payment of claims. These services include risk management services, claims processing services, and legal services. Insurance buyers may also receive certain financial advantages associated with insurance, particularly those that are tax-related.

Risk Management Services. Because they are extensively involved with the insured losses of many different policyholders, insurers develop expertise in recognizing and controlling exposures to loss. This expertise is especially important for exposures to high severity, low frequency losses, which are the greatest concern of insurance buyers. Insurers are able to provide assistance both in identifying loss exposures and in recommending ways by which these exposures might be financed or controlled. Naturally, insurers and their representatives have a financial incentive to help insurance buyers identify exposures that can be insured. But insurers' risk management services have a much greater impact than their role in facilitating insurance sales. Because insurers bear the immediate impact of loss, they have strong financial incentives for identifying and implementing measures that control losses. Insurers' loss control services are provided to businesses as a service when insurance coverage is written, and insurers' loss control representatives may work directly with policyholders with the mutual goal of controlling losses.

Loss control services and other risk management services can be separately purchased from brokers, risk management consultants, or other service organizations. An extra degree of confidence may be added when such services are provided by an insurer who also underwrites the coverage. An insurer provides these services not only as a service to clients, but also to benefit the insurer who is directly affected by the results of those services.

Claims Services. Because they are extensively involved with the insured losses of many different policyholders, insurers develop expertise in handling claims. Settling claims or suits, administering the paper flow associated with claims payment, and preventing fraud in the process are among the activities that are challenging, to say the least, for those without special expertise in the field. Like risk management services, claims services can be purchased from independent claims handling services. However, the insurer may have a stronger incentive to control claims costs because of its direct accountability for making loss payments.

Many claims, especially liability claims, require the attention of attorneys having special expertise. Insurers not only develop such expertise, but they also develop a network of legal resources over a large geographic area, for the benefit of policyholders with widespread operations.

With liability insurance, an insurer's claims services interject an outside party between the claimant and the insured. This sometimes is advantageous in that it reduces stresses on other relationships between two parties that may need to continue to cooperate in other matters. A clear example involves workers compensation claims and the potential for conflict between worker and employer. The conflict may be buffered when it is an insurer, rather than the employer, that negotiates agreement on some issues of a claim.

Tax Benefits. Insurance premiums are tax deductible when the premium is paid, while retained losses are tax deductible only when the loss is paid. Funds set aside in reserve for retained claims to be paid in the future are not deductible from income tax. Although loss dollars must eventually be paid and may eventually be deductible, losses may be uneven and unpredictable from year to year, while premium payments may be much more predictable and consistent. These features, in turn, may result in lower long-term tax liabilities with insurance than with retention.

Drawbacks to Insurance

Although insurance presents a number of advantages over retention or other means of financial losses, it is not without its problems or difficulties. The additional costs associated with administration, moral and morale hazards, and adverse selection must be added to pure loss costs transferred to the insurer. For some potential insurance buyers, these costs are high enough to preclude the purchase of insurance and to select other alternatives instead. For insurers, these costs can mean the difference between profitability and insolvency.

Administrative Costs. If the cost of transferring the risk of potential losses to an insurer is the same as the expected cost of retained losses, most individuals would purchase full insurance protection. Insurance would enable the individual to shift from a position of uncertainty to one of great certainty without paying anything more than the amount of expected losses which otherwise would be borne anyway.

Of course, it does not work that way in practice. In addition to the costs of expected losses, the insurer needs to charge an additional amount to cover its expenses of doing business. This additional charge reflects costs the insurer expects to incur in marketing insurance, administering claims, and developing a fair return on equity. As these costs increase, the individual or corporation becomes less likely to purchase full insurance, although partial insurance may still be considered. If these additional charges are perceived to be too high, alternatives to insurance may be used instead. These include techniques such as exposure avoidance, loss prevention, loss reduction, noninsurance transfers, and retention.

The insurer has to manage carefully the tradeoffs between the increased profitability that accompanies higher insurance premium charges and the loss of customers that might result as insurance buyers select other risk management alternatives.

Adverse Selection. If an insurer charges a premium reflecting the average expected losses of the members of a group, those with higher-than-average risks of loss will have a greater tendency to purchase insurance than those presenting lower-than-average risks. Insurance that is priced according to the average risk will seem a bargain to those with high exposures, and it will seem unduly expensive to those with low exposures.

Adverse selection results from the inability of each insurer to measure with complete accuracy the loss exposures associated with each individual exposure. Simply increasing premium levels to compensate for adverse selection will not always solve the problem. In fact, high premium levels can lead to even greater adverse selection: Those with lower-than-average risks may find other insurers who are willing to provide their insurance at a favorable cost, leaving only the higher-risk insurance buyers to purchase the high-priced insurance. Many of the problems associated with insurance markets and price regulation are rooted in problems related to the difficulty of measuring the risks associated with each individual applicant and the adverse selection that may result from a mismatch between exposures and premium levels.

The role of insurance underwriters is to minimize adverse selection. This is done by differentiating among applicants for insurance, determining which are acceptable and which are unacceptable, and properly pricing each policy.

Moral and Morale Hazards. Once insurance protection is made available, the behavior of the insured may change. Because the insured does not directly bear the full financial impact of insured losses, he or she may change the amount of resources spent in controlling losses. Insurers have long recognized the need to monitor the activities of their policyholders to ensure that exposures do not change once the premium has been paid. To the extent that moral and morale hazards cannot be controlled, it is necessary to reflect their impact in insurance premium levels. It also can be very important to structure insurance contracts in a way that provides insurance buyers with some incentives for loss control.

TYPES OF INSURANCE

Insurance is a very important part of most risk management programs. The remainder of this chapter describes the most commonly used insurance coverages or policies. Emphasis here is placed on the use of insurance as a risk management tool for dealing with certain loss exposures. The objective is to explain the general purpose and the broad scope of each coverage, rather than concentrating on policy details. Every insurance policy has specific detailed exclusions, limitations, conditions, and miscellaneous provisions that are not addressed in this overview.

Insurance coverages can be divided into four broad categories:

- *Property insurance* addresses property loss exposures. More specifically, it covers accidental losses resulting from damage to or loss of the property of the insured or other property in which the insured has an insurable interest. When a loss has occurred, the insurance company settles the claim by paying the insured-claimant according to the terms of the contract. Insurance covering the building owner against fire damage to the owner's building is an example of property insurance.

- *Liability insurance* addresses liability loss exposures. The insurer generally agrees to defend the insured against liability claims that may be covered and to pay damages directly to a third-party claimant, usually on behalf of the insured, if the insured is proven to be legally liable for injury or damage to the claimant. Auto liability insurance, for example, defends liability claims against an insured driver brought by other parties who are injured by that driver's allegedly negligent driving and pays any settlements or awards.

- *Health (accident and sickness) insurance* is designed to protect individuals and families from financial losses caused by accidents and sickness. Some limited health insurance policies, such as those available to commercial airline passengers, school children, or athletic team members, cover only injuries resulting from certain specified types of accidents. *Medical expense in-*

surance policies pay for the cost of medical care, including hospital and doctor bills and other bills for health care services, whether the medical expenses were incurred because of accidental injury, sickness, or disease. *Disability income insurance* pays periodic benefits to replace the lost income of insureds who are unable to work as a result of accident or sickness.

● *Life insurance* pays, upon the death of the insured, a specified sum to the beneficiary named in the policy, or it may distribute the sum under an optional alternative to lump-sum payment. Many "cash value" life insurance policies not only provide death benefits but also include a savings element.

Although this text concentrates on property and liability insurance, some property-liability insurance policies include health- and life-insurance-like coverages.

The property-liability insurance field can also be subdivided into *personal lines insurance*, covering individuals and families, and *commercial lines insurance*, covering businesses and other organizations. The distinction is not always clear-cut. Borderline cases may include insurance on smaller farms, smaller apartment buildings, and larger pleasure boats. Especially for such borderline cases, the distinction between "personal lines" and "commercial lines" coverages often depends on the reason for making the distinction. One major reason involves the question as to which person or department in an insurance office will handle a particular type of coverage.

PERSONAL LINES INSURANCE

Personal lines property and liability insurance includes those coverages usually purchased by one individual or by a group of related individuals who make up a household. Obvious examples are homeowners policies and auto policies, which address most of the insurable property and liability loss exposures faced by a typical household. Other personal lines insurance policies, not mentioned here, deal with specialized exposures, such as those relating to hobby items or high-risk activities.

Homeowners Insurance

A homeowners insurance policy includes property insurance, liability insurance, and a form of limited third-party accident insurance. Because it includes, packaged in a single policy, several coverages that otherwise could be written separately, it is considered a "package policy." Although a variety of homeowners policies have been developed by insurance service organizations and specific insurance companies, most follow generally the same format. As explained shortly, one major difference among homeowners policies relates to the number of perils covered under the property insurance section.

Property Coverage. The property coverage is provided in Section I of the homeowners policy. The exposures treated by the property coverages of the homeowners policy can be broken down by property, perils, and consequences.

Covered Property. Section I of the homeowners policy covers property loss exposures involving loss, damage, or destruction to the following property item(s):

- The dwelling building (Coverage A)
- Other structures—such as a detached garage (Coverage B)
- Personal property (Coverage C)

Some types of property, such as autos, aircraft, or animals, are not covered. Other types, such as money, watercraft, or business property, are subject to sublimits (maximum limits applicable to loss to that type of property). And coverage for some types of property, such as jewelry and furs, is subject to sublimits when the cause of loss is theft.

Tenants' and condominium unit-owners' homeowners policies are available for those who occupy rented property or own condominium units. The distinguishing feature of these variations is that they do not include coverage for the dwelling building housing the living unit. Other variations of the homeowners policy are available for owners of mobilehomes.

Covered Perils. A choice of one of two or three different versions of the homeowners policy usually is available for those who own and occupy their home, providing different levels of coverage in terms of the number of perils covered under the policy.

- The *basic* homeowners policy, now discontinued in most states, covers against damage to the dwelling building, other structures, or personal property by a dozen or so of the most significant perils ("fire," "windstorm and hail," and so forth) specifically listed and described in the policy.[2]
- The *broad* homeowners policy, which is a little more costly, covers against loss by a longer list that includes another half dozen (or so) perils that include such causes of loss as water leaks, falling objects, and weight of ice, sleet, or snow.
- The *special* homeowners policy covers the building and other structures against "risks of loss" that are not otherwise excluded, an approach that covers even more causes of loss than

the broad form. This often is referred to as "all-risks" coverage, although the term is somewhat misleading. Only the perils listed in the policy are excluded; all others are included.

Under the special homeowners form, covered perils for *personal* property are the same as under the broad form. However, an endorsement often is available to cover personal property on a "risks not excluded" basis.

Covered Loss Consequences. The loss consequences covered under the homeowners policy include both "reduction in value" and "extra expense to replace" covered dwelling property, as well as the cost of debris removal. The "extra expense to replace" the dwelling building or other structures is automatically included within the homeowners policy's "replacement cost" coverage. Replacement cost coverage on personal property often is available as an option at extra cost; otherwise, personal property is covered only for its actual cash value.

Another loss consequence is covered by the *loss of use coverage*, provided under Coverage D of the homeowners policy. This coverage reimburses an individual or family for its *additional living expense—* the extra expense of daily living, such as the cost of living in a motel and eating meals out, while the damage to covered property, by a covered peril, is being repaired. The homeowner may instead elect coverage for the *fair rental value* while the home is not fit to live in because of the damage to property.

Exclusions and Limitations. Like all property-liability insurance policies, a homeowners policy contains many exclusions and limitations. For example, certain types of property—such as money, jewelry, and furs—are subject to a sublimit limiting coverage to a specified dollar amount. Certain perils are also excluded, most notably flood and earthquake. Specified policy limits clarify the maximum amount payable for building(s), other structures, personal property, and loss of use claims.

Liability Coverage. Section II of the homeowners policy provides, under Coverage E, coverage against liability loss exposures relating to *bodily injury* to the person of others or *property damage* to the property of others for which the insured may be held legally responsible because the damage or injury arose out of the insured's activities or out of a condition on the insured premises. The insurer agrees to defend the insured against such claims at the insurer's expense. Although the legal costs of a defense can be high, many claims are successfully defended with the result that the insured is not obligated to pay any damages to the claimant.

The insurer also agrees to pay, up to the applicable limit, covered damages arising out of a judgment or an out-of-court negotiated settlement against the insured. These damages are paid directly to the injured claimant, on behalf of the insured.

Even though most claims related to intentional acts, business activities, autos, aircraft, and watercraft are subject to exclusions written into the policy, homeowners policies cover a wide range of liability loss exposures. It must be emphasized that coverage applies only to claims alleging bodily injury or property damage arising out of the insured's premises or activities. Claims for damages arising out of sexual harassment or discrimination, for example, would not fall within the scope of this liability coverage. Neither would claims unrelated to either the covered premises or to activities of the insured, or claims for which the insured is not legally responsible to pay damages.

Medical Payments to Others Coverage. Coverage F of Section II of the homeowners policy provides for medical payments to *persons other than the insured* or residents of the insured's household who are injured on the insured's premises or in connection with the insured's activities. Because there is no requirement that the insured be legally obligated to pay damages to the injured person, this actually could be considered a form of accident insurance. Because coverage can be applied by the insured whether or not there is any negligence, wrongdoing, or "fault" by the insured, it also is a form of no-fault insurance.

Medical payments to others coverage typically is subject to a nominal limit, such as $1,000 per person. While it will not pay any large medical bills, it meets a need by enabling insureds to see that first-aid bills are taken care of when a guest is injured, even if the guest has merely stumbled over his or her own feet. Claims like this are tricky, because the insured often feels a duty as host to "take care of" a guest's injuries—even when no *legal* duty exists. In cases of this type, insureds often are tempted to admit at least some small degree of liability in causing the guest's injury, so that the host's insurance coverage will be invoked. In the face of this temptation, insureds sometimes breach ethical responsibilities to deal with the insurer with the "utmost good faith." Attempts to defend the insured against liability in such claims can be difficult at best.

When injuries to guests are involved, the medical payments coverage helps the insured to preserve good will. By enabling the insurer to pay small medical bills without determining fault, the medical payments to others coverage also serves a valuable role in eliminating some liability claims. When small claims are handled under the medical payments coverage, no defense costs are involved because it is not necessary to determine legal responsibility. If the claim escalates, the insured has not yet admitted any responsibility and a normal defense can be mounted.

Personal Auto Insurance

Some of the typical family's most significant loss exposures result from ownership, maintenance, or use of an auto. Some are property exposures, such as the potential reduction in value of one's auto following a collision with another auto or object. Others are liability exposures, such as the possibility of causing bodily injury to pedestrians or passengers of other autos, or the possibility of accidentally causing damage of another's auto.

Personal auto insurance is designed for individuals and families who own private passenger autos. A widely used standard personal auto insurance policy is the personal auto policy (PAP) developed by Insurance Services Office (ISO). This is the policy discussed here. By far, the majority of homeowners losses involve property losses, although homeowners liability claims can involve large dollar amounts. In dollar amounts, auto liability claims far exceed physical damage claims (which generally are limited by the value of the covered auto). Moreover, liability insurance is compulsory in most states, while physical damage exposures often are retained, especially for older vehicles with a relatively low value.

Personal auto policies do more than insure the loss exposures relating to one described vehicle ("covered auto") and its named driver. Subject to exclusions and limitations, liability and property insurance generally "follows the car," even when unlisted drivers are operating it. Insurance also "follows certain drivers," even when driving autos not described in the policy, such as new, borrowed, or rented autos. The many cases in which more than one policy could apply are addressed by specific policy provisions beyond the scope of this chapter.

Liability Coverage. Under the PAP's Part A—Liability Coverage, an insured is protected in the event of a claim or suit for bodily injury or property damage arising from an accident involving a covered auto. Most liability claims result from collisions, but bodily injury resulting when a vehicle slips off a jack, or property damage to clothing cut by a piece of sharp trim, is also within the scope of coverage.

Bodily injury is defined as "bodily harm, sickness or disease, including death that results." Property damage is defined as "physical injury to, destruction of or loss of use of tangible property." Unless a liability claim alleges bodily injury or property damage, as defined, coverage is not activated.

Liability coverage responds principally to the insured's liability to others for "bodily injury" and "property damage" incurred under tort law. Other forms of legal responsibility—for example, liability assumed under a contract—are also within the scope of the auto liability coverage.

No-fault statutes, where they apply, may limit the circumstances under which injured parties may sue a motorist who causes them to become injured in an auto accident. An effective no-fault statute can therefore reduce the frequency of auto liability claims. Whether or not a no-fault statute applies, an insured is protected against liability claims for bodily injury or property damage brought by third parties.

Medical Payments Coverage. The primary purpose of the PAP's medical payments coverage is to provide prompt reimbursement for medical expense when insureds or other persons are injured while occupying a covered auto or when the named insured and family members are injured as pedestrians. Like the medical payments to others coverage of the homeowners policy, the medical payments coverage of the personal auto policy serves to limit the number or size of claims by injured passengers. A major difference, however, is that the homeowners coverage does not apply to injuries *to* the insured and family members, while the auto coverage does.

Under the PAP's Part B—Medical Payments Coverage, related medical expenses are covered if incurred within a three-year period after the date of an auto accident.

Both the liability coverage and the medical payments coverage can apply to some of the same elements of a loss—particularly those involving passengers in a vehicle driven by a driver who is at fault in an accident. In that sense, the medical payments coverage relates closely to the liability coverage. However, medical payments coverage applies regardless of fault. In that sense it can be considered a form of accident insurance.

In states with a no-fault statute, medical payments coverage may be replaced or supplemented with *personal injury protection* coverage, which provides broader benefits not based on fault. The benefits may include disability benefits (wage-loss replacement), payment for substitute services (babysitter to substitute for injured parent), funeral benefits, and other specified benefits, which vary from state to state.

Uninsured Motorists Coverage. Uninsured motorists coverage is unique to auto insurance, and it is difficult to categorize by comparison with other types of insurance. Uninsured motorists coverage is designed to provide a source of recovery to insureds who are involved in an auto accident caused by either an unidentified hit-and-run driver or an identified motorist who does not have auto liability insurance. In theory, this coverage should not be necessary in most states because compulsory insurance laws require all motorists to carry liability insurance. In practice, however, many motorists succeed in evading compulsory insurance laws or are out-of-state drivers. The motorist can, of course, be sued, but many uninsured motorists have few assets available to pay a judgment.

Under Uninsured Motorists Coverage, Part C of the PAP, the injured person's insurer agrees to pay *directly to the insured* those damages that the injured person is legally entitled to recover from the owner or operator of an uninsured motor vehicle for bodily injury caused by an accident. This payment is not made on behalf of the uninsured motorist who is responsible for the damages, but the effect is about the same for the claimant/insured.

For an insured to collect uninsured motorists coverage, the uninsured driver must be legally liable to pay damages. Coverage does not apply in the absence of fault. Uninsured motorists coverage therefore has some but not all characteristics of third-party liability insurance (liability is required to trigger coverage, but it is another party's liability) and some characteristics of first-party coverages, such as property insurance or health insurance (the insured collects from his or her own insurer, but only if the responsible party has no insurance).

A number of states have statutes that extend this coverage to include not only bodily injury, but property damage as well.

Another variation, available in many states, is *under*insured motorists coverage. This coverage applies when the at-fault motorist has auto liability insurance with limits that at least meet the applicable state financial responsibility or compulsory law requirements but are less than the insured's own limits of *under*insured motorists coverage.

Property Insurance (Physical Damage) Coverage. Part D of the PAP, Coverage for Damage to Your Auto, provides insurance coverage for physical damage to a covered auto. Covered causes of loss are provided in two categories—"collision" and "other-than-collision" (comprehensive):

- The collision coverage applies only to loss resulting from collision. *Collision* is defined as the upset of an auto or its impact with another vehicle or object. This is the most common cause of substantial damage to autos.
- The phrase *other-than-collision* includes all nonexcluded perils other than collision that cause accidental or direct loss to an auto.

"Other-than-collision" coverage often is available without purchasing collision coverage, but collision is not available unless "other than collision" also is purchased.

Coverage applies to the reduction in value of the auto caused by the collision or other peril. When it is so badly damaged that it is not worth repairing, an auto is considered a "constructive total loss." The insurer typically pays the full value of the "totaled" vehicle, after applying any deductible, to the vehicle owner in exchange for the right to recover any salvage value. The insurance company usually then sells the wrecked vehicle to a salvage yard for its scrap value.

When an auto is stolen, its use value is reduced to zero from the perspective of the owner. The result is the same as with an auto that has been "totaled," except that there is no salvage (unless the missing auto is recovered).

The amount payable by the insurer under Part D is limited to (1) the "actual cash value" of the damaged or stolen property, or (2) the amount required to repair or replace it—whichever is less. The actual cash value of an auto generally is considered to be its retail before-loss value in the used car market. When repair is not feasible (or when the car has been stolen), the amount the insurer pays, plus the deductible, should be sufficient for the insured to buy another used car of similar age and condition.

Transportation Expenses Coverage. When a car is damaged, destroyed, or stolen, the owner often incurs an additional loss consequence, beyond the reduction in value of the vehicle itself, in the form of extra expenses to rent a temporary substitute, or to pay for public transportation, until the vehicle is replaced, repaired, or recovered. The personal auto policy provides coverage, up to a stated amount per day and a stated maximum dollar amount, to rent a replacement car, beginning forty-eight hours after the theft, when the entire vehicle has been stolen. Similar coverage applicable to losses caused by collision or other perils is available as an option at additional cost.

Other Personal Lines Insurance

The homeowners and auto policies provide protection for the most common property and liability loss exposures faced by the typical household. Other personal lines policies are available to meet some of the needs that cannot be addressed through homeowners and auto policies.

Dwelling Policies. Dwelling policies are available for the owners of tenant-occupied homes or others who are not eligible for coverage under a homeowners policy. These policies can provide essentially the same property coverage as a homeowners policy but provide no liability coverage (unless it is added in an optional endorsement).

Personal Liability Coverage. Personal liability coverage, similar to the liability coverage of homeowners policies, is available as an endorsement to a dwelling policy or in a separate policy for those who desire the coverage but do not have a homeowners policy. There is no significant difference from the comparable coverage in homeowners policies when personal liability coverage is provided in a separate policy.

Personal Inland Marine Floaters. The supplementary property insurance most commonly used by households and individuals is an inland marine form known as the *personal articles floater*. When attached to a homeowners policy, it is known instead as a *scheduled personal property endorsement*. The personal articles floater (PAF) policy provides coverage on one or more of nine optional classes of personal property—jewelry, furs, cameras, musical instruments, silverware, golfer's equipment, fine arts, and rare and current coin and stamp collections.

To some extent, the coverage available in a personal articles floater may overlap with coverage also available in the homeowners policy. However, some types of property that are subject to dollar sublimits in the homeowners policy can be insured for their full value under an inland marine floater. An inland marine floater usually also provides coverage against loss by more perils than the homeowners policy. For example, Jonathan's homeowners policy does not exclude coverage for musical instruments. However, he purchased a personal articles floater specifically describing his guitar, selecting an amount of insurance equal to its value, and providing coverage against those perils not excluded. Coverage for a loss caused by accidentally sitting on Jonathan's guitar would be provided by a personal articles floater, but not by an unendorsed homeowners policy.

Personal Umbrella Policy. The purpose of personal umbrella policies is to protect individuals and families against those rare high-severity liability claims that may exceed the coverage available under a personal auto policy or a homeowners policy.

Sold with coverage limits of $1 million or more, personal umbrella policies provide broad "excess" liability protection—protection over and above the liability coverage provided by other personal policies providing liability coverage. In addition, personal umbrella policies also cover some liability exposures that may not be included in "underlying" liability policies, such as coverage for claims alleging damage by libel and slander. For these later coverages, the umbrella policy "drops down" so as to provide coverage over a relatively modest (such as $250) retention (similar to a deductible).

Watercraft Policies. The loss exposures connected with the ownership and use of watercraft are quite similar to those involving an auto.

As a property exposure, a boat can represent a considerable investment that may be reduced in value through physical damage or destruction. Watercraft and their motors, trailers, equipment and furnishings can be lost, damaged, or destroyed by perils on land, as well as the so-called perils of the sea. Perils of the sea include the forces of wind and waves, and collision with submerged objects as well as with fixed objects such as docks, piers, and wharves. Loss also can come about by the perils of stranding, sinking, capsizing, lightning, fire, explosion, earthquake, flood, and theft.

As for liability exposures, watercraft also can expose to loss the personal assets of persons who may be held liable for injury or damage to others in a boat accident.

Those insureds who find homeowners watercraft coverage inadequate can choose from among a variety of watercraft insurance policies including outboard motor and boat policies, watercraft package policies, and personal yacht insurance policies.

COMMERCIAL PROPERTY AND LIABILITY INSURANCE

Businesses and other organizations face a wide array of property and liability loss exposures, many of which can be insured. This section describes the more common types of commercial property and liability insurance.

"Commercial Property" Coverage

The most widely used property insurance forms insure property loss exposures arising out of buildings and personal property at fixed locations. ISO applies the label "commercial property" to this series of insurance policy forms—a usage that is somewhat confusing because other types of insurance policies also provide coverage on business (commercial) property. Quotation marks around the phrase "commercial property" when referring specifically to this particular series of ISO policies are intended to minimize confusion.

A complete "commercial property" policy must include both a "property coverage" form and a "causes-of-loss" form, as well as some additional documents. The property coverage form describes the property and loss consequences covered, while the causes-of-loss form describes the perils for which coverage applies.

Causes-of-Loss Forms. The same causes-of-loss forms can be used regardless of the type of property or loss consequences covered. The causes-of-loss forms used with the various "commercial property" forms describe the perils for which coverage applies and include the basic form, the broad form, and the special form. Like the homeowners forms, the broad and special "commercial property" causes-of-loss forms provide coverage against successively more perils.

- The *basic* form lists eleven perils such as fire, lightning, and explosion.
- The *broad* form adds four more perils to the list.
- The *special* form covers "risks of direct physical loss" not specifically excluded or limited by the form, sometimes referred to as "all-risks" coverage.

Earthquake (more specifically, the "earth movement" peril) is not a covered peril under these forms. However, a separate causes-of-loss form may be added, when desired, to add earthquake coverage. Flood coverage also is excluded; flood coverage often is available under a separate government-sponsored program or, sometimes, through a so-called difference in conditions (DIC) insurance policy.

Building and Personal Property Coverage Form. The building and personal property coverage form (BPP), when accompanied by a causes-of-loss form and other essential documents, is designed to address the standard fixed-location building and/or contents loss exposures of most commercial insurance buyers. It serves a key role in most property programs, and many other property coverages are best analyzed by comparison with it.

The BPP makes available coverage on three optional categories of property:

- *Buildings* must be specifically described in the declarations. Building(s) coverage includes not only the structure but also permanently installed fixtures, machinery, and equipment as well as personal property, such as lawnmowers and garden hoses, used to maintain or service the building.
- *Personal property of the insured* includes furniture and fixtures, machinery and equipment, stock, and all other personal property owned by the insured and situated on the premises, as defined.
- *Personal property of others* applies to personal property on premises in the custody of the insured, such as customer-owned appliances that are being repaired.

Although all three coverages are printed in the building and personal property coverage form, each coverage applies only when a dollar limit of insurance for that coverage is shown on the declarations page at the front of the policy. The declarations page also indicates which causes-of-loss form applies to which coverage. It is possible, for example, for the special causes-of-loss form to apply to the coverage on the building, while the broad causes-of-loss form applies to personal property of the insured.

Covered loss consequences under the standard building and personal property coverage form include reduction in value of the property (actual cash value basis coverage) and coverage for the cost of debris removal. Coverage for the "extra cost to replace" property can be provided through the popular "replacement cost" option, written into the policy but applicable only when the coverage is activated as indicated in the policy's declarations page.

Business Income Coverage Form (BIC). When property is lost, damaged, or destroyed, activities that use that property often must be discontinued. For example, a small shoe store may close completely for two months following a fire. At other times a partial shutdown is involved—the body shop of an auto dealership may be closed following an explosion in the service bay, while other sales and servicing activities continue. These two examples illustrate conditions leading to a total or partial loss of income during the period of shutdown.

In another case, suppose the showroom of an auto dealership is destroyed by a fire although other buildings are unaffected. The dealership might continue sales operations by bringing in a tent and a mobilehome to serve as a temporary showroom and office. In this situation the business would continue to produce income, but it would incur extra expenses to do so. Many similar situations are possible, some involving a combination of lost income and extra expense.

The BIC addresses the loss exposures relating to *loss of income* and/or *extra expense to operate*. The elements of the loss exposure covered by the basic business income coverage form are as follows:

- *Property*—damage to or destruction of real or personal property at the described premises
- *Perils*—caused by a covered cause of loss
- *Consequences*—loss of business income (as defined) resulting directly from the necessary interruption or partial suspension of business

Actually, there are two versions of the BIC. The so-called "business income coverage form (and extra expense)" covers an additional consequence—extra expenses incurred to avoid or minimize a suspension of business. The other business income coverage form, "business income coverage form (without extra expense)," covers extra expenses only to the extent that they reduce the amount of the business income loss. The cost of the tent used as an auto showroom might qualify under this provision to the extent that sales would have dropped without renting the tent.

Boiler and Machinery Coverage

Any organization using steam boilers and other pressure vessels is exposed to the possibility that the vessel could explode. Electrical and mechanical devices can break down in other ways, depending on the nature of the device. An accident to boilers and machinery can damage the boiler or machinery itself, and it can also damage the building housing the boiler, personal property in the building, and other nearby buildings and their contents—depending on the severity of the explosion. Without a boiler or a critical machine, the business may also be interrupted resulting in a loss of income or extra expenses to continue in operation.

In theory, all boiler- and machinery-related exposures could be insured along with the building and contents. In practice, however, boiler and machinery coverage is handled as a separate line of insurance and the coverage available in a boiler and machinery policy is excluded under a "commercial property" policy. The reason is that loss control activities are vitally important in connection with boilers and machinery. In fact, most boiler and machinery losses are prevented because insurers' periodic inspections uncover and correct problems before they lead to a loss. Therefore, boiler and machinery insurance tends to be first a loss control service and, secondly, insurance for those unusual situations in which a loss occurs despite preventive measures. The bulk of the insurance premium dollar goes to pay the expenses of the loss control service.

Most states have laws requiring periodic inspections of boilers and pressure vessels by a licensed inspector. In many states, boiler insurers' loss control representatives are licensed as deputy inspectors for the state, and their inspections meet the requirements of the law.

The boiler and machinery coverage form dovetails with the BPP. While the BPP emphasizes a certain category of covered property, the boiler and machinery coverage form concentrates on certain causes of loss. Although the BPP and associated causes of loss forms do not exclude coverage for damage to boilers and machinery by windstorm, fire, or other covered perils, they do exclude coverage for certain causes of loss—such as boiler explosions and sudden breakdowns of machinery, including electrical arcing and centrifugal force.

In general, boiler and machinery insurance is available to provide coverage for damage to boilers, machinery, buildings, and personal property by these other perils, including the reduction in value of covered property as well as any associated loss of business income.

Commercial Crime Coverage

"Commercial property" insurance provides coverage for some crime losses. However, the "commercial property" insurance coverages previously mentioned exclude or severely restrict coverage for loss to money and securities. In addition, except for the special form, the "commercial property" causes of loss forms do not provide coverage for loss by theft. Both of these types of coverage are the (not necessarily exclusive) province of commercial crime insurance.

Property subject to criminal loss includes all kinds of real and personal property, but money, securities, jewels, and other compact valuable items are especially susceptible. The major consequence of a crime loss usually is the loss of the property itself. Partial losses occur when only a portion of exposed property is stolen. Consequences such as loss of income, or extra expenses to operate, also may be involved when raw materials, merchandise, or other property necessary for the firm's operations has been stolen, or when the "scene of the crime" has been roped off by police.

Because they are treated differently by insurance policies, crime exposures can be divided into two categories: (1) crimes committed by outsiders (burglary, robbery, and so forth), and (2) crimes committed by employees (employee dishonesty).

Over a dozen different commercial crime coverages are available on ISO forms. The coverages vary in terms of the covered property (for example money and securities, or property other than money and securities), covered locations of property, or covered perils. The perils insured with crime insurance include employee dishonesty, forgery, robbery, burglary, theft, computer fraud, and extortion.

In terms of loss consequences, crime insurance deals almost entirely with the value of the lost property. Coverage against loss of income or extra expenses normally is not provided in standard crime forms. However, loss of business income caused by theft could be insured under a business income coverage form to which the causes-of-loss—special form applies. An organization that faces a substantial business income exposure caused by theft of property should consider this arrangement of coverage.

Ocean Marine Policies

Many businesses and organizations are involved in the import and export of goods requiring transport across the oceans of the world. Many materials are also shipped on inland waterways, lakes, rivers, and canals, or by oceangoing vessels traveling among domestic ports. Various vessels carry cargo, vehicles, and passengers; serve the fishing industry; drill for oil and gas; and help to build and maintain marine facilities all over the world. Tugboats provide essential assistance to larger vessels and move barges on waterways. The use of private pleasure boats also has increased dramatically in recent years. Property and liability exposures arising out of these various activities can be insured with ocean marine insurance.

Some of the same perils that threaten property on land also threaten waterborne commerce. For example, vessels and cargoes are subject to loss by perils such as fire, lightning, and windstorm. However, the hazards to waterborne shipping go well beyond those affecting land transportation. For a ship, there is the complex interaction between the wind and the water, and the ship may strike rocks or shoals. Physical damage or machinery malfunction that would be minor ashore could be disastrous to a ship. For example, a hole in the side of a building may be a minor problem, while a hole in the side of a ship could very well mean the total loss of the ship. Goods shipped by water are subject to loss due to such things as the corrosive effect of salt water, moisture damage, and the pitching and rolling of ships.

Ocean marine insurance policies are classified as hull, cargo, and protection and indemnity (P&I) policies. A hull policy provides coverage for the hull of the ship, materials and equipment, and stores and provisions for the officers and crew. Also included are the machinery, boilers, and fuel supplies owned by the insured. Ocean marine hull insurance contracts also contain some important liability insurance coverage called the "collision" or "running down" clause. This clause covers liability for damage to other ships and their cargoes from collision involving the insured vessel.

Cargo in ocean commerce means only property for which a freight charge is paid and thus does not include the personal effects of passengers and crew of a ship. Cargo can be covered for named perils or on an "all-risks" basis, and protection can apply to only a single voyage or to all the voyages of a shipper through an open cargo policy.

P&I provides liability coverage. Damage to shore and waterway installations and bodily injury to persons including employees and passengers are covered as well as damage to cargo being carried. The P&I policy also covers the insured shipowner's or operator's liability for fines that may be imposed for violation of laws. If the ship is sunk and constitutes a hazard to navigation, the cost—which can be quite expensive—of raising, destroying, or removing the wreck is also covered by P&I insurance.

Commercial Inland Marine Policies

Inland marine insurance, as an outgrowth of ocean marine insurance, provides coverage for exposures to merchandise in transit, bailee exposures, exposures to "floating" property, and several other types of property exposures.

Inland marine policies include those covering property while in transit or in the custody of bailees, "floating" property, specified types of dealer policies, property sold on a deferred payment basis, instrumentalities of transportation and communication, and electronic data processing equipment.

- Coverage for property in transit (such as goods aboard a truck) is available to the property owner. Coverage also is available for the carrier to cover its potential liability to the property owner if the property is lost, damaged, or destroyed.
- A bailee (such as a dry cleaner) is liable under common law for loss to property in the bailee's custody only when the loss is due to the bailee's negligence. However, to preserve their goodwill, many business firms purchase insurance for the benefit of customers regardless of the circumstances of the loss. This is referred to as bailees customers insurance.
- Contractors equipment floaters are inland marine insurance policies used to cover mobile articles, machinery, and mobile equipment including equipment used by contractors when constructing such things as buildings, highways, and dams.
- Installation floaters are used to cover loss to materials and equipment that are in transit to a construction site, that are at the construction site before being incorporated into the building, and that have been installed in a structure until such time as the installation is complete and has been accepted by the owner of the property.
- Dealers policies, such as so-called jewelers block policies, cover stock while on the premises of a jeweler, in transit, or otherwise off premises.
- Inland marine insurance can be written to cover property purchased on a deferred payment basis, such as a piece of machinery that is leased or purchased on an installment basis.
- Inland marine policies also can cover fixed property that is an instrumentality of transportation or communication, such as bridges, tunnels, and communication towers.
- Some inland marine forms cover losses related to electronic data processing equipment, including physical loss to the hardware as well as extra expenses to operate and business interruption. Although electronic data processing equipment is not excluded under the personal property coverage of commercial property forms, inland marine forms usually are better suited to provide coverage. Inland marine forms may cover perils such as mechanical breakdown, which is excluded under "commercial property" forms.

Inland marine insurance can provide very broad coverage of perils as well as flexibility of policy forms and rates. There may be a great deal of variation from one insurer's policy to the next, and there often is ample opportunity for both the insurer and the insured to negotiate coverage and pricing terms to suit specific needs.

Aviation Insurance

Except for their obvious three-dimensional character, aviation exposures generally resemble the down-to-earth exposures facing motor vehicles and watercraft. Both property and liability exposures are involved, and the major hazards involve their use as a means of transport. Aviation insurance, for the most part, is written in package policies providing both property and liability coverages. One major difference is a limitation of coverage to pilots who must meet certain stated qualifications; auto and watercraft policies generally insure any potential driver, even a totally unqualified one.

Aircraft physical damage insurance, also called aircraft hull insurance, protects the insured against loss involving physical damage to the insured aircraft. It is written on an "all-risks" basis and may apply only while the aircraft is on the ground (coverage may or may not include taxiing), or it may apply both while the aircraft is on the ground and in flight. Aircraft liability insurance is designed to cover the tort liability exposures of aircraft owners and operators. It provides protection against third-party claims alleging bodily injury or property damage arising out of an insured's ownership, maintenance, or use of aircraft. Medical payments coverage similar to that provided by auto policies also is available.

Commercial General Liability Coverage

Businesses and other organizations face liability exposures arising out of their premises and operations in progress, as well as liability exposures related to their products and completed operations. Other liability exposures are assumed under written contracts or agreements.

ISO commercial general liability (CGL) forms are available to cover these types of exposures by providing the following three coverages:

1. *Bodily injury and property damage liability.* This covers liability for bodily injury and property damage related to the premises and operations of the insured, including operations performed by subcontractors and products and completed operations liability unless specifically excluded. Various related coverages are included, such as contractual liability and liability for small, nonowned watercraft.

2. *Personal injury and advertising injury liability.* This covers liability for such offenses as libel, slander, false arrest, malicious prosecution, and some advertising offenses.
3. *Medical payments.* This coverage is a no-fault type of accident coverage similar to that described previously for homeowners insurance. It applies to the medical expenses incurred by others as a result of accidental bodily injury on the insured's premises or arising out of the insured's off-premises operations in progress.

The CGL excludes coverage for many exposures that are covered by other policies, such as those related to aircraft, autos, owned watercraft, and certain types of professional activities (such as coverage for a physician's error in the treatment of patients, or an architect's design error, for example). Other exclusions eliminate coverage for exposures covered by workers compensation and employers liability policies, discussed later. One important exclusion of the CGL is for pollution exposures, including any liability for cleanup mandated by the government. Insurance may be provided on a separate pollution liability coverage form. However, insurance companies are very selective in screening those for whom they will provide pollution coverage.

Business Auto Coverages

The exposures covered by a *personal* auto policy, such as reduction in value, loss of use, and liability to others were discussed previously. For a business or organization, these exposures can be covered by a business auto coverage form. The unendorsed business auto coverage form fits only the basic needs of most businesses. The basic provisions of the business auto form offer only two coverages, liability and physical damage. If other coverages are either required by law, such as personal injury protection (no-fault), or selected voluntarily, such as medical payments or uninsured motorists coverage (which also can be mandatory), endorsements must be attached to the business auto form.

Garage and Truckers Coverages

Both garages (a category that includes auto sales and service stations, parking garages, and the like) and trucking companies face auto-related loss exposures similar to those covered by the business auto coverage form. However, the exposures and insurance needs are distinctive to the extent that unique coverage forms are needed.

The most distinctive aspect of garages—auto dealers, service stations, and others—is that, because of the nature of their operations, it is difficult to distinguish between their auto liability and general liability exposures. The garage policy combines auto and general liability insurance into a single form that also may include auto physical damage coverages, as well as "garagekeepers" liability coverage for damage to customers' autos in the garagekeeper's care, custody, or control.

Truckers—those in the business of transporting goods for others—are subject to many regulations that may develop special insurance needs. In addition, practices such as interchanging trailers with other truckers lead to special coverage needs that are not adequately addressed by the business auto coverage form.

Workers Compensation and Employers Liability Insurance

State workers compensation statutes make an employer liable for the payment of medical expenses, weekly compensation for lost wages, and other benefits to a worker injured on the job. The employer is responsible whether or not the injuries were caused by the employer's negligence—in other words, on a no-fault basis. To finance this liability exposure, most employers purchase workers compensation insurance. In fact, most employers are required by law to purchase this insurance. However, a number of large employers, whose workers compensation dollar losses are fairly predictable from year to year, meet an alternative legal requirement by arranging a retention program out of which benefits are paid to, or on behalf of, injured employees. When a retention program is used, "excess insurance" often is purchased—and it may be required by the state—to "kick in" in the event of a major loss.

As mentioned, coverage for exposures related to employees usually is provided by the workers compensation and employers liability policy, which actually includes two coverages.

- *Workers compensation* coverage is governed by the applicable state statutes and pays those amounts the employer is required to pay for medical expenses, weekly compensation, and other benefits such as death benefits.
- *Employers liability* coverage protects employers from employment-related suits separate and distinct from claims for workers compensation benefits. Although workers compensation provides the sole remedy for most claims resulting from employee injuries, there are some exceptions. Details are beyond the scope of this chapter.

Professional Liability Insurance

Physicians, surgeons, and other medical professionals face substantial professional liability exposures. Other medical professionals who have been held liable for negligence are dentists, optometrists and opticians, pharmacists, anesthetists, physical therapists, and nurses. Hospitals and other institutions providing medical care also are subject to professional liability exposures.

Professional liability exposures also are faced by other professionals, including accountants, architects and engineers, attorneys, and insurance agents and brokers. Claims against these professionals typically allege an error or omission in rendering, or failing to render, professional services.

Professional liability insurance policies cover professional liability imposed on insureds because of acts, errors, or omissions in the conduct of their profession. Coverage does *not* apply to losses arising out of hazards usually covered by general liability insurance, such as bodily injury resulting from a wet floor or other conditions on the premises.

Directors and Officers Liability Insurance

Corporate directors and officers may be sued for a breach of corporate duties. Directors and officers liability exposures arise under both common and statutory law. For example, directors and officers have a duty to exercise reasonable care in the performance of their corporate functions and, under the Securities and Exchange Act of 1934, have a duty to disclose facts that are material to stockholders, bondholders, and potential investors. Directors and officers may be individually liable for their own torts or jointly and severally liable for the tortious acts or omissions of another agent of the corporation. When a director or officer is a defendant in a lawsuit, most states permit or require that the corporation provide indemnification for costs incurred in the suit.

A directors and officers legal liability insurance policy, commonly referred to as a D&O policy, provides coverage for wrongful acts for any individual director or officer or a group of directors and officers. It is divided into two parts: The first covers directors' and officers' individual liability when they are not indemnified by the corporation, while the second part indemnifies the corporation if it has paid money to directors and officers for expenses associated with a claim.

Excess and Umbrella Liability Insurance

Excess and umbrella liability policies for commercial insureds are similar in concept to personal umbrella insurance discussed previously. An excess liability policy sits over one or more other liability policies (primary policies) and effectively increases the insured's limits of liability by providing similar coverage to that provided by the primary policies. An umbrella policy, which also sits over one or more primary policies, also provides broader coverage than that provided by the primary policies.

For example, an umbrella policy may sit over several primary policies; a commercial general liability policy, a business auto policy, an aviation policy, and the employers liability section of a workers compensation policy. It could provide coverage at least as broad as these other policies in all areas and provide broader coverage in some areas such as personal injury and property damage. Minimum limits of primary insurance may be required, such as a minimum of $1 million for commercial general liability, and a self-insured retention normally applies to those areas not covered by the primary policies.

Businessowners Policies

Like households, various small businesses have essentially the same types of property and liability exposures; they therefore have similar insurance needs. Like homeowners policies, businessowners policies use an approach under which the insured purchases a set of prearranged property and liability coverages on a virtually all-or-nothing basis, with relatively few options or alternatives. The process involves relatively few risk management decisions.

Those eligible to purchase businessowners policies include small office, mercantile, and service businesses, as well as condominium associations and owners of apartment houses.

The businessowners program offers property coverage on buildings or personal property of the insured or both, depending on whether the business is a landlord, a tenant, or an owner-occupant. The two businessowners property coverage forms—standard and special—differ primarily with respect to the covered causes of loss. Buildings and personal property are covered on a replacement cost basis, which includes not only the reduction in value but also the extra cost to replace. Other covered loss consequences include debris removal, loss of business income, and extra expenses. Several fringe coverages are also included, and others are available as options.

The liability coverage of the businessowners policies is essentially the same as that of the CGL.

The benefits of using a businessowners policy are ease of handling, streamlined rating procedures, and a reduced need for detailed risk management decisions. By purchasing a businessowners policy, many insurance buyers receive a more complete set of coverages than they would if each coverage was separately purchased. A disadvantage is that the businessowners program does not offer the range of options available when coverages are purchased separately, and businesses may overlook unusual insurance needs that require special attention.

Farm Policies

The typical family farm involves an indivisible combination of personal and business exposures. The personal exposures are essentially the same as those faced by a nonfarm family as typically covered by a homeowners policy. The property and liability exposures arising out of agricultural operations, on the other hand, resemble those of other businesses but also have unique characteristics relating generally to crops, animals, and equipment.

Farm insurance policies may be configured in a number of ways. Although farm property is separately described and insured, other property coverages in the typical farm policy closely resemble the coverages of a homeowners policy (except for the coverage on other structures). And the liability coverage encompasses both personal and business liability arising out of claims for bodily injury and property damage.

Surety Bonds

A contract of suretyship is an agreement whereby one party agrees to be answerable for the debt or default of another. Such a contract involves three parties—the principal, the obligee, and the surety. The principal, also known as the obligor, is obligated to perform in some way for the benefit of the obligee or creditor. The surety guarantees to the obligee that the principal will fulfill the underlying obligations. In most cases, the party making the guarantee—the surety—is an insurance company that also writes property-liability insurance.

To enhance the practical value to others of a principal's legal obligation to perform, an insurer guarantees the performance of the obligation—and backs its guarantee with its own name, reputation, and financial resources—under an enforceable written instrument called a surety bond. In return, the insurer is compensated by the premium it charges for the bond.

The exposures insured under a surety bond are very different from those discussed in the other parts of this chapter. They consist of the possibility that one party will fail to do something, such as complete a work contract or pay taxes to the government. The obligee who has the exposure does not purchase insurance to cover the exposure, but instead requires the obligor to purchase a surety bond. This requirement can be thought of as a form of loss control. The insurance company will not issue the surety bond until it is comfortable that the obligor is in a position to meets its obligations. From the point of view of the obligee, requiring the obligor to purchase a surety bond is a form of noninsurance transfer of its exposures.

SUMMARY

From the perspective of the risk manager, insurance is one of several tools for dealing with loss exposures. A loss exposure presents the possibility of a loss. Property loss exposures involve three elements—the item, the peril, and the loss consequences. Liability loss exposures, on the other hand, focus on the possibility that a claim for damages might be made. Property and liability exposures differ from one another in respect to both measurability and timing of loss payments.

The risk management process involves the following four steps:

- Identifying and analyzing loss exposures
- Selecting the best risk management technique(s)
- Implementing the decision
- Monitoring the program

Insurance is only one of the techniques usable in risk management. Others mentioned in this chapter are as follows:

- Exposure avoidance
- Loss prevention
- Loss reduction
- Separation of loss exposures
- Duplication
- Noninsurance contracts
- Retention

The best technique (usually a combination of techniques) can be selected through cost/benefit analysis, taking into account nonfinancial considerations as well as financial costs.

Not all exposures are insurable. Ideally, an insurable exposure possesses the following characteristics:

- Pure risk
- Uncertainty as to probability or time of loss
- Definite happening, time, and amount
- Large number of insured exposures
- Loss not simultaneously affecting many insureds
- Economic feasibility

In addition to payment of claims, insurance often provides ancillary benefits. Its drawbacks include administrative costs, adverse selection, and moral and morale hazards.

This chapter's overview of the most common personal and commercial property and liability coverages demonstrates the range of exposures that can be treated by insurance.

Chapter Notes

1. Alice Ann R. Head and George L. Head, "On Risk Management: The Power of Politics in Safety," *National Underwriter* (Property & Casualty), July 22, 1991, p. 17.
2. The exact number of perils may vary from one policy edition to the next.

CHAPTER **3**

Regulation and Insurance

One cannot delve very deeply into the study of insurance without recognizing that insurance practices, products, and prices are strongly influenced by regulation. This chapter views insurance from the perspectives not only of insurers, but also of regulators and the public. Members of these groups often do not agree among themselves, much less with members of other groups. This chapter treats a number of sensitive issues by presenting a range of speculative opinions and relatively few hard facts. The approach is descriptive rather than prescriptive. The goal is to present an objective view of the strengths and weaknesses of contemporary insurance regulation, one that fairly captures various perspectives without generally adopting an editorial position.

This chapter includes a discussion of the reasons for government regulation, various means of regulation, the major areas that are regulated, and an analysis of the state versus federal regulation issue. It also considers the role of the government as an insurer.

REASONS FOR GOVERNMENT REGULATION OF INSURANCE

Private insurers are regulated primarily by the states, but they also must comply with numerous federal laws and regulations.

Primary Goals of Insurance Regulation

Insurers are regulated primarily for the following reasons:

- To maintain insurer solvency
- To protect policyholders
- To avoid destructive competition

Although these objectives clearly overlap, each will be separately discussed.

Maintain Insurer Solvency. A fundamental purpose of insurance regulation is to maintain the solvency of insurers. This objective, also referred to as *solidity,* emphasizes the ways in which the regulatory process attempts to maintain and enhance the financial condition of private insurers.[1] Solvency regulation is important for the following reasons:

- *Future protection.* Premiums are paid in advance, but the period of protection extends into the future. If insurers become insolvent, future claims may not be paid, and the insurance protection paid for in advance may be worthless. To ensure that insurers are financially able to pay their claims, the financial condition of insurers must be carefully monitored.
- *Public interest.* Solvency regulation is justified because insurance is a business affected with a public interest. Large numbers of individuals and the community at large are adversely affected if insurers become insolvent.
- *Money held in trust.* Insurance companies hold tremendous sums of money in trust for the ultimate benefit of policyholders. Government regulation is necessary to safeguard such holdings.

Insurance companies have become insolvent despite regulatory reviews aimed at the preservation of solvency. However, sound regulation should minimize the number of insolvencies.

Protect Policyholders. Regulation is necessary because of the complex and technical nature of insurance contracts. Insurance contracts are legal documents containing many complicated and interrelated clauses, exclusions, and limitations, and most policyholders are not insurance experts. Without regulation, some insurers might draft insurance contracts that were inappropriately narrow and restrictive.

Insurance regulation also helps to protect consumers against fraud and unethical market behavior by insurers and their representatives. Although most insurance personnel are ethical, there are exceptions. Some consumers have been sold insurance that was not needed. Some insurance producers have misrepresented the nature of coverage in order to make a sale. Some insurers have engaged in unfair claims practices, refusing to pay legitimate claims or unfairly reducing the amounts paid. Dishonest and inept insurance managers have contributed to the insolvency of a number of insurers. Regulation can protect policyholders against such abuses.

Avoid Destructive Competition. At times, some insurers underprice their products to increase market share at the expense of competitors' market shares. This practice drives down price levels in the market as a whole. When market rate levels are inadequate, some insurers may become insolvent; others may withdraw from the market or restrict their writings of new business. As a consequence, an insurance shortage may develop, and individuals and firms may be unable to obtain needed coverages. Certain types of insurance may be temporarily unavailable at any price.

To avoid destructive competition, regulators have the responsibility of determining that premium levels are adequate. When insurers engage in destructive price cutting, the result can be the insolvency of some insurers or a severe contraction in the insurance market to the detriment of the public.

Other Goals of Insurance Regulation

In addition to the primary goals discussed above, insurance regulation has several related goals:

- To ensure appropriate and equitable rates
- To make insurance available and affordable
- To enforce insurance laws
- To keep the public informed on insurance matters

Ensure Appropriate and Equitable Rates. Policyholders are treated fairly when insurance rates are both appropriate and equitable. Appropriate insurance rates are not inadequate—inadequate rates would threaten insurer solvency, nor are they excessive—excessive rates would exploit policyholders. Equitable rates, in short, are fair. Rate regulation is discussed in detail later in this chapter.

Make Insurance Available and Affordable. Regulators may attempt to make certain types of insurance more readily available, especially those that tend to be considered necessities. For example, all states have restrictions on the rights of insurers to cancel or nonrenew auto insurance policies. These restrictions are intended in principle to promote availability by making continuous coverage available to policyholders. In practice, however, they may also lead to increased rejections of new business applications. Insurers are reluctant to develop unbreakable long-term relationships with some insurance buyers, whose exposures they would like to reconsider periodically.

To keep insurance from becoming unavailable, regulators at times have restricted the right of insurers to withdraw from certain markets or geographical territories, or they have imposed penalties on insurers seeking to withdraw. This situation arises from time to time, in connection with personal auto insurance, when one or more insurers has announced an intention to discontinue this line of coverage in a state where it believes the rate levels authorized by regulatory authorities are inadequate.

Affordability has often been an issue with workers compensation, professional liability, and other lines of insurance. However, the affordability issue has been especially prominent with personal auto insurance in states where rates have soared because of high claims costs, defects in the legal system, and numerous other factors. In these areas, many motorists, especially low-income drivers, are unable to afford auto insurance (or are unwilling to pay the high cost of insurance that adequately reflects their exposures to loss).

Regulators often take actions intending to make insurance more affordable. In states requiring rate approval, regulators may, for example, grant rate increases that insurers consider inadequate or may, in some cases, require insurers to reduce their rates. In response to inadequate rate levels, insurers may reduce the volume of new business they are willing to write, with the result that a regulatory measure intended to promote affordability conflicts with the availability goal.

Besides simply restricting rate levels, another approach to affordability is to require a rating classification system that has the effect of subsidizing one group at the expense of another. For example, motorists in certain cities may complain that their auto insurance rates are too high. In response to these complaints, rating territories may be broadened—instead of having separate rating territories for city drivers and rural drivers, the revised rating territory might include both groups. The result helps city drivers who then pay lower rates. Their premium reductions are offset by the rural drivers who pay higher rates.

In addition to regulating rates, governments may make insurance more widely available and affordable by providing government subsidies to private insurers, by enacting government insurance programs, or by creating residual market programs, all of which are discussed later in this chapter.

Enforce Insurance Laws. State insurance departments have the primary responsibility for enforcing various insurance-related laws and regulations. State insurance departments employ a variety of personnel to help enforce the law, including not only insurance specialists but also attorneys, accountants, and actuaries.

Keep the Public Informed on Insurance Matters. Insurance regulators strive to keep the public informed on insurance matters. Typical activities include publishing shoppers' guides to auto, homeowners, and life insurance; issuing press releases on new insurance laws and regulations; providing claims filing advice following a natural disaster; and numerous other activities of an informational or educational nature. The investigation of consumer complaints serves not only to protect policyholders, but also to inform them of their rights and duties.

MEANS OF REGULATING INSURERS

All states have laws that regulate the activities of private insurers. Among other things, various state laws regulate the formation of insurers, capital and surplus requirements, licensing of agents and brokers, investment of funds, financial requirements for maintaining solvency, insurance rates that can be charged, marketing and claim practices, taxation of insurers, and the rehabilitation or liquidation of insolvent insurers. Although it has no direct authority, the National Association of Insurance Commissioners (NAIC) has a profound effect on state insurance regulation.

In addition, a wide variety of legislation has been enacted at both the state and the federal levels to protect the rights of consumers. Examples include restrictions on the right of insurers to cancel and laws designed to make certain types of insurance more widely available and affordable.

State Insurance Departments

Insurers are regulated by state insurance departments that have the primary responsibility for enforcing the various insurance laws and regulations.

Nature of the Office. Each state, as well as the District of Columbia, has an insurance department or bureau. The state insurance department is headed by an insurance commissioner or director who is either appointed by the governor or elected by the public. While most commissioners are now appointed, the trend is toward making them answerable directly to voters.

While some states have strong and effective insurance departments that protect policyholders and regulate insurers in an effective manner, other states fall short of this goal.

A study of the General Accounting Office (GAO) argued that state insurance regulation is not characterized by an "arms-length" relationship between regulators and the regulated but is dominated by "revolving door"[2] commissioners. A high percentage of commissioners are employed in the insurance industry before they enter public office, and many are employed by insurers after leaving office. Moreover, the GAO charged that NAIC advisory committees are dominated by insurer representatives.

In rebuttal, the state insurance commissioners deny they are overly responsive to private insurers. Commissioners frequently regulate in ways objectionable to the industry, such as issuing cease-and-desist orders, fining or penalizing insurers for infractions of the law, forbidding insurers to engage in mass cancellations, limiting rate increases, and taking numerous other actions that benefit policyholders at the expense of insurers.

As to some insurance regulators' previous insurance employment, it is noted that the expertise necessary to understand insurance operations well enough to regulate effectively can most likely be found in a person who has previously worked in the insurance industry.

Sources of Funding. State insurance departments are funded in part from revenues derived from state premium taxes, audit fees, filing fees, and licensing fees, but premium taxes are the major source of revenue. Premium taxes are designed primarily to raise revenues for the states; they are not allocated specifically for insurance regulation. Although state premium taxes are substantial, only a relatively small amount of the taxes collected is spent on insurance regulation, averaging only 6 percent of the revenues collected.[3]

Insurance Department Activities. A typical state insurance department engages in a wide variety of regulatory activities, including the following:

- Approving policy forms
- Holding rate hearings and reviewing rate filings in prior approval states
- Licensing new insurers
- Licensing agents and brokers
- Investigating policyholder complaints
- Rehabilitating or liquidating insolvent insurers
- Issuing cease-and-desist orders
- Conducting periodic examinations of insurers by field examiners, including claims and underwriting audits
- Evaluating solvency information
- Performing market conduct examinations
- Fining insurers in violation of state law
- Publishing shoppers' guides and other consumer information (in some states)

The activities listed above require a high level of professional skill and expertise. However, according to the Government Accounting Office the level of professional training represented on department staffs is relatively low, especially in actuarial science; state insurance departments spend relatively little to upgrade the skills of professional staff members; salaries are relatively low compared to the salaries qualified professionals can earn elsewhere; and the turnover of state insurance commissioners is relatively high.[4] The states vary widely in the amount of money spent to carry out their activities. Some states spend substantially more money on regulation than others that have about the same population and premium volume.

National Association of Insurance Commissioners

The National Association of Insurance Commissioners (NAIC) by itself has no direct regulatory authority. However, it has a profound impact on the nature and uniformity of state regulation.

The NAIC was formed in 1871. Originally called the National Convention of Insurance Commissioners, the NAIC meets periodically to discuss important industry problems and issues in insurance regulation.

The NAIC assists state insurance departments through model laws and regulations and through the sharing of financial information about insurers. In addition, the NAIC has developed uniform financial statements that insurers must file with the states.

Model Laws and Regulations. The NAIC periodically drafts model laws and regulations in important areas. A *model law* is a draft bill for consideration by state legislatures, which may adopt it with or without modification. A *model regulation* is a draft of a regulation that may be implemented by a state insurance department upon passage of the model law. Model laws and regulations are *models* that individual states may or may not choose to follow. The laws and regulations of many states follow at least the main idea of NAIC models, resulting in some degree of uniformity among the states. Examples of model laws include model legislation establishing a statutory fire insurance policy, and a model property and liability insurance rating law.

Sharing Financial Information. The NAIC provides important financial information to the states on insurers that are potentially insolvent. For example, several years ago the NAIC conducted a financial analysis of 4,910 insurers licensed to do business in the United States. The analysis used sophisticated methods to identify insurers with financial problems. A team of senior examiners from different states analyzed the financial results. For each insurer, the information was then sent to the state where the insurer was domiciled and to all states where the insurer did business. A task force also monitors the actions of the state in dealing with the financial problems that have been identified.[5]

Federal Regulation

An ongoing issue is whether insurers should be regulated by the states or whether some or all regulation should be shifted to a federal agency. Arguments often are heard that the McCarran-Ferguson Act, discussed in Chapter 1, should be repealed or modified by federal regulation. Counterarguments are heard insisting that McCarran-Ferguson must be retained.

The major arguments for federal regulation of insurers are as follows:

1. *Federal regulation can provide complete uniformity in regulation among the various states.* Insurers doing business in more than one state currently are confronted with differing laws, regulations, and administrative rules. Under federal regulation, laws and regulations would be uniform. With only one set of laws, regulations, and administrative rules, insurers might have lower expenses.
2. *Federal regulation would be more efficient.* Insurers doing business nationally would deal with only one federal agency instead of fifty-one different insurance departments. Also, a federal agency might be less likely to yield to industry pressures from local or regional insurers. Another advantage given is that federal regulation might be relatively less expensive than state regulation.
3. *Federal regulation could attract higher-quality personnel.* If adequately funded, higher salaries and prestige would attract higher-quality personnel who would do a superior job in regulating insurers.

On the other hand, opponents of federal regulation present the following arguments:

1. *State regulation is responsive to local needs.* Conditions vary widely among the states, and state regulators can respond quickly to local problems and needs. In contrast, federal regulation and government bureaucracy would result in considerable delay in solving local problems.
2. *Uniformity of state laws can be attained through the NAIC.* As a result of the model laws and regulations of the NAIC, there is reasonable uniformity in state laws at the present time, with due weight given to local circumstances and conditions.
3. *Greater opportunities in innovation are possible.* State regulation allows innovations in regulation to be tried without harm to the rest of the country. An individual state can experiment with new approaches to regulation. If that approach fails, only

that state is affected. In contrast, federal regulation would affect all states if a new approach fails to meet its objectives.

4. *State regulation is already in existence, and its strengths and weaknesses are known.* In contrast, the benefits and possible adverse consequences of federal regulation on the insurance industry are unknown.

5. *State regulation results in a desirable decentralization of political power.* In contrast, federal regulation would increase the power of the federal government and dilute states' rights.

AREAS OF REGULATION

Insurance regulation focuses mostly on the following areas:

- Formation and licensing of insurers
- Licensing of insurance personnel
- Solvency regulation
- Rate regulation
- Contract regulation
- Market conduct

Each of these areas is discussed in some detail in the following sections.

Formation and Licensing of Insurers

An *admitted insurer* is one that is licensed by the state insurance department to do business in that state. In contrast, *nonadmitted insurers* can legally operate only through the mails or only by marketing insurance that cannot be obtained from an admitted insurer. Nonadmitted insurers that attempt to sell, through personal contacts, insurance that is available on an admitted basis, may be subject to civil or criminal penalties.

A license indicates that the insurer has complied with the state's insurance laws and is authorized to write certain types of insurance. The issuance of the license indicates that the insurer meets minimum standards of financial strength, competence, and integrity. If this evaluation later changes, the license can be revoked.

Domestic Insurers. After becoming organized, an insurer must be licensed (authorized to transact business) in its home state where it is considered a *domestic* insurer. A domestic insurer's license generally has no expiration date. An insurer must secure a separate license to operate in any state other than its state of domicile, and it will operate in other states as a *foreign* (domiciled out-of-state) insurer. The license secured by a foreign or *alien* (domiciled out-of-country) insurer generally has to be renewed annually.

Domestic insurers almost always are organized under general statutes of incorporation. The organizers must meet the conditions imposed on corporations engaged in noninsurance activities plus some special conditions imposed on insurers. The organizers file an application for a charter that states the names and addresses of the incorporators, the name of the proposed corporation, the territories and lines of insurance in which it plans to operate, the total authorized capital stock (if any), and its surplus. The state insurance commissioner reviews the application to see whether the proposed insurer also meets the state's special licensing requirements.

Capital and Surplus Requirements—Stock Insurers. An insurer must be financially sound. State laws require that *domestic stock insurers* satisfy certain minimum capital and surplus requirements before a license will be granted. The *capital stock account* represents the value of the shares of stock issued to stockholders. *Paid-in surplus* represents the amount paid in by stockholders in excess of the par value of the stock. For example, the minimum capital requirement may be $1 million with paid-in surplus equal to 50 percent of the capital amount. Capital and surplus requirements vary widely among the states with respect to amounts and lines of insurance written.

In a stock insurer, the sum of the capital account and paid-in surplus (plus any voluntary reserves) is frequently referred to as *policyholders' surplus*. For regulatory purposes, policyholders' surplus is important for the following three reasons:

1. The amount of new business an insurer may write is limited by the amount of policyholders' surplus.
2. Policyholders' surplus is needed to offset any substantial underwriting or investment losses that might occur.
3. Policyholders' surplus can be used to offset any deficiency in loss reserves that may occur over time.

In most states, the initial capital and surplus requirements do not depend on the premium volume the insurer intends to write. However, the minimum requirements can vary, according to the lines of insurance the insurer offers to the public. For example, to write fire insurance, an insurer might be required to have a specific minimum capital and surplus. For each additional line of insurance the insurer intends to write, the dollar requirement increases. For a multiple-line insurer planning to write all kinds of insurance except life insurance, most states impose a lower capital and surplus requirement than the sum of the requirements for the separate lines.

State capital and surplus requirements have been criticized on the following grounds:

1. The capital and surplus requirements for stock insurers vary widely among the states.
2. Many states have very low minimum requirements.
3. States may not relate the amount of capital and surplus to the premium volume to be written.
4. Economic conditions may change the adequacy of a fixed dollar requirement.

One study showed that the maximum ratio of premiums to capital and surplus that can be safely written varies depending upon the insurer's size, the lines of insurance written, and economic conditions. The authors of the study concluded that a statute should be enacted that allows the state insurance commissioner greater judgment in establishing the minimum capital and surplus requirements.[6] As this text went to press, NAIC committees were attempting to develop "risk-based capital standards," which would relate an insurer's reported statutory surplus to the risks inherent in its overall operations.

Surplus Requirements—Mutual Insurers. Because a *mutual insurer* has no capital, the minimum requirement applies only to surplus. The initial surplus may be derived from premium deposits paid by would-be policyholders; a portion of the initial surplus may be borrowed. Most states require that mutuals have an initial surplus equal to the minimum capital and surplus requirement for stock insurers writing the same lines of business. Some states, however, have set a minimum surplus requirement for mutuals that is lower than the minimum capital and surplus requirement for stock insurers.

To organize a mutual, in many states it is also necessary to have applications and deposit premiums from a stated minimum number of persons on more than a stated number of separate exposures with aggregate premiums in excess of a certain amount. The purpose of this requirement is to provide the insurer with a minimum book of business, and hence some stability, the day it opens its doors.

Other Requirements. In addition to tests of financial strength, states often impose other formation or licensing requirements. For example, the proposed name for a mutual insurer must include the word "mutual," and the proposed name of any new insurer must not be so similar to that of any existing insurer that it would be misleading. The commissioner may have the authority to refuse a license if he or she believes the incorporators or directors of the insurer are untrustworthy. Some states even permit the commissioner to deny a license to an otherwise worthy applicant if he or she believes that there is no need for additional insurers in the state. Once the license is issued it can be revoked if the insurer operates in a manner that is clearly detrimental to the welfare of its policyholders (for example, consistent failure to pay legitimate claims or fraudulent business conduct).

Foreign and Alien Insurers. To be licensed in a particular state, foreign (out-of-state) insurers first must show they have satisfied the requirements imposed on them by the state in which they are domiciled. Second, foreign insurers must generally satisfy the minimum capital and surplus and other requirements imposed on domestic insurers by the state in which they wish to do business.

Alien (non U.S.) insurers must also satisfy the requirements imposed on domestic insurers by the state in which they desire to be licensed. In addition, alien insurers usually must establish a branch office in some state and have funds on deposit in the United States equal to the minimum capital and surplus required.

Nonadmitted Insurers. Under surplus lines laws, a nonadmitted insurer may be permitted to transact business through agents or brokers if (1) the insurance cannot be obtained after the insurance buyer has made a diligent attempt to secure the protection from admitted insurers, (2) the nonadmitted insurer is "acceptable," and (3) the agent or broker has a special license authorizing him or her to place such insurance. The surplus lines agent or broker usually must be a resident of the state.

An "acceptable" nonadmitted insurer generally must file a financial statement that the commissioner finds satisfactory, appoint the commissioner as an agent to receive service-of-process in the state, obtain a certificate of compliance from its home state or country, and, if an alien insurer, maintain a trust fund in the United States. Some states leave the determination of acceptability to the agent or broker. A few states permit brokers or agents to use other nonadmitted insurers if the desired insurance cannot be obtained from either admitted or "acceptable" nonadmitted insurers.

Risk Retention Act. This discussion of the formation and licensing of insurers would not be complete without mentioning the Risk Retention Act. Congress enacted this law to make products liability and commercial liability insurance more readily available to business firms.[7]

The Product Liability Risk Retention Act of 1981 provided for the formation of risk retention groups and insurance purchasing groups in the areas of products and completed operations liability. The 1986 amendments expanded and renamed the 1981 Act to include all areas of commercial liability, except workers compensation. To facilitate their operation, the Liability Risk Retention Act exempts both risk retention and purchasing groups from many of the state laws that normally apply to private insurers.

Risk Retention Groups. A *risk retention group*, a special type of insurance company enabled by the Risk Retention Act, must be chartered and licensed as a liability insurer under the laws of at least one state. The group can then write insurance in all states. It need not obtain a license in a state other than its chartering state. However, in a nonchartering state, a risk retention group may be subject to some state laws including the following:

- Unfair claim settlement practice laws
- Premium taxes
- Membership in joint-underwriting or similar associations, where insurance companies share losses in such areas as assigned risk auto insurance.

Purchasing Group. A purchasing group is, as the name implies, a number of insurance buyers who purchase insurance together. A purchasing group operating under the Risk Retention Act has access to some special rights or privileges. An insurer insuring a purchasing group is exempt from most state laws requiring approval of rates or policy forms. A purchasing group also is not subject to any "fictitious group" laws designed to preclude the formation of a "group" under some pretext when the real purpose behind the group's existence is to make it possible for members to purchase insurance on a group basis. Such laws may require a group to have been in existence for a certain period of time or require a group to have a certain minimum number of members in order to purchase insurance as a group.

A purchasing group must be made up of persons or entities with like exposures and in a common business. However, this definition is vague and will probably lead to disputes as to its exact meaning. For example, it is likely that the definition would include a group of dentists. But would it encompass a group of landlords involved in both residential and commercial buildings?

Regulatory Concerns. State regulators have expressed concerns about potential problems regarding the financial security of liability insurance purchased under the Liability Risk Retention Act of 1986, particularly when the risk retention providing the coverage is chartered in another state. Congress went some distance in meeting these concerns by allowing the chartering state to request (and to implement, if necessary) an examination of the financial condition of a group even when the commissioner has no reason to believe that the group is financially impaired. However, some state regulators still remain fearful of abuses under the Act, and some advocates of the risk retention group concept remain concerned about the possibility of overregulation.

Licensing of Insurance Personnel

Another important area of insurance regulation is the licensing of those who sell insurance, give insurance advice, or represent insurers. These groups include producers (agents and brokers), insurance consultants, and claims adjusters.

Agents and Brokers. Agents and brokers must be licensed in each state in which they do business. Insurance producers operating without a license are subject to civil, and sometimes criminal, penalties.

All states require these insurance producers to pass an examination or examinations. The examinations are administered by the state insurance department or by an independent organization that contracts with the state to provide this service. The states differ according to the degree of difficulty and number of exams an applicant must pass in order to sell all types of insurance. Some states require a specified number of hours of approved training before the licensing exam can be taken. Some states excuse applicants from the licensing examination if they have earned the CPCU professional designation. Applicants also may be excused if they have taken an exam similar to the department exam after completing an approved course. Some states have reciprocal agreements in which the exam is waived for agents or brokers who have met the licensing requirements in other states. A model NAIC licensing bill requires an examination but excuses CPCUs from all parts of the property and liability insurance examinations except those dealing with the rules, regulations, and laws of the particular state; many states have adopted this approach.

The term of the license generally is one or two years. The license can be renewed by payment of a fee and satisfaction of any state continuing education requirements. The majority of states now require a certain number of approved continuing education credits to be earned during some time period (such as two years) as a condition for retaining an insurance license. Continuing education credits can be earned in a variety of ways, including taking CPCU courses and passing their national examinations, attending short seminars, attending professional meetings, and so on. The continuing education requirements encourage agents and brokers to maintain or upgrade their professional skills and knowledge. In addition, the continuing education requirements help ensure at least a minimum level of competence and improve overall the quality of insurance activity in the state. They also serve to eliminate marginal insurance producers.

Virtually all states have *countersignature laws* that require property and liability insurance contracts insuring residents of the state to be signed by a resident agent licensed in the state. Many states require that the resident agent must be paid some fraction of the total commission, even if the resident provides no service to any of the parties.

Agents and brokers are subject to fines, penalties, or revocation of their license if they engage in certain illegal and unethical activities. An agent may be penalized for engaging in practices that are in violation of the state's *unfair trade practices act.* The insurance commissioner has the power to suspend or revoke an agent's license because of dishonesty or fraud, misrepresentation, or unfair discrimination. For example, a dishonest agent might embezzle premiums paid by the policyholders or might appropriate some claims funds. An agent also might misrepresent the policy to a client. For example, *misrepresentation* of the losses that are covered by an insurance contract may induce a client to purchase that contract under false pretenses. *Twisting* is a special form of misrepresentation in which the agent or broker induces a policyholder through misrepresentation to replace one contract (usually life insurance) with another to the detriment of the insured. *Unfair discrimination* is any act that favors· one insured unfairly over others.

An agent can also be penalized for rebating. Rebating is currently illegal in all but two states. *Rebating is the practice of giving a portion of the producer's commission or some other financial advantage to an individual as an inducement to purchase the policy.* Rebating is especially problematic with life insurance policies for which the agent's first year's commission is sizable.

Rebating was the first form of unfair discrimination to be prohibited by law in an 1886 Louisiana statute. Rebating also is prohibited in unfair trade practices acts. If an agent rebates part of the commission to one policyholder but not to another, that act is considered unfair discrimination. If the agent rebates the same percentage of the commission to all policyholders, that act is not unfairly discriminatory, but it is still illegal.

States that issue a separate broker's license may use a different set of examinations to test the competence of candidates, or they may establish higher standards for the broker's license than the agent's license. Some states prohibit persons from taking the broker's examination until they have been licensed agents for a specified period, such as two years.

A *surplus-lines agent or broker* must first be licensed as an agent or broker. In most states, the only additional requirement is the payment of a fee and the posting of a surety bond that guarantees the surplus-line agent will pay the state premium tax on the nonadmitted insurance. Some states administer a special examination program for surplus-line agents or brokers.

Insurance Consultants. Some states require insurance consultants to be licensed. *An insurance consultant is an individual who gives advice, counsel, or an opinion concerning insurance contracts sold in the state.* Separate examinations usually are required to be an insurance consultant in both life and health insurance and in property and liability insurance.

Licensing requirements for a consultant's license vary among the states. A state may impose stricter requirements for a consultant's license than for an agent's or broker's license. For example, in Nebraska, an applicant for a consultant's license must either (1) be licensed as an agent or broker, or as a consultant in another state, for three years preceding the date of application or (2) successfully complete a specific program of study that has broad national or regional recognition as determined by the director of insurance. In addition, insurance consultants must meet certain continuing education requirements.

Finally, certain occupations are exempt from the licensing requirement as an insurance consultant. Depending on the state, the exempt groups include the following:

- A licensed agent who gives advice incidental to the normal course of the agent's insurance business and does not charge a fee other than commissions from insurance sold
- An actuary, attorney, certified public accountant, insurance instructor, or trust officer of a bank who consults during the normal course of business and the consulting is incidental to such business.
- A person employed as a risk manager who consults to the company in which he or she is employed during the normal course of full-time employment.

Claims Adjusters. Some states require the licensing of claims adjusters representing insurance companies. Licensing of claims adjusters is justified because of the complex and technical nature of insurance contracts and to protect claimants from unfair, unethical, and dishonest claims practices. The licensing of claims adjusters provides some assurance that adjusters will be aware of prohibited claims practices, that minimum technical skills will be demonstrated, and that policyholders will be treated fairly.

Public adjusters (who represent insureds for a fee) generally are required to be licensed. Again, the objective is to ensure technical competence and protection of the public.

Solvency Regulation

One of the highest priority areas in insurance regulation currently is solvency regulation. The financial strength of insurers must be carefully monitored to ensure their ability to pay covered losses.

The amounts held by insurance companies can be very large (particularly when compared to the wealth of individual insureds) and the time between payment and receipt of funds can be many years. It is therefore particularly important for the insurer to be viewed as credible. A portion of its credibility arises from the insurer's ability to price and control properly the risks that it assumes.

The insurer, if it is to survive and prosper, must operate efficiently. Like any other investor, it must constantly seek the highest return while taking into account the degree of risk that it faces in all of its markets. Through a combination of competition in price, quality of services offered, and flexibility, insurers can offer the products demanded by insurance consumers at the lowest possible price. The attempt to compete in terms of price and service leads to the survival of the most efficient insurers while less efficient insurers will be replaced. Indeed, in competitive markets, only those insurers who are able to provide the desired products at the lowest possible price (while still able to cover their costs) will survive and prosper. Other insurers will not be able to earn a competitive return on the resources used in the production of insurance services. If the firm cannot reorganize its resources in a way that provides a more efficient utilization, it will eventually experience bankruptcy (and a forced reorganization) or the resources (human, physical, and capital) will be sold.

While the possibility of bankruptcy of an insurer always exists, insurers must maintain the public confidence that all losses will be paid. Particularly for the interests of individual consumers and small businesses not having sophistication to analyze the claims-paying ability of an insurance company, it is essential to maintain a high degree of solvency in the insurance industry as a whole. State regulation, independent rating bureaus, and state-sponsored insurance guarantee funds all help protect the consumer. Competition among insurance agents and brokers (who have a vested interest in the long-term relationships with the consumer), can also help consumers avoid some problems with purchasing insurance from more risky firms. Unfortunately, none of these systems is foolproof.

Methods to Ensure Solvency. Four principal methods are used to ensure solvency and measure the financial strength of insurers:

- Financial requirements
- Review of financial statements

- Insurance Regulatory Information System
- Onsite field examinations

Financial Requirements. To maintain their solvency, insurers must meet certain minimum financial requirements, such as minimum capital and surplus requirements, restrictions on investments, and valuation of loss reserves. Each insurer must meet such requirements to obtain and keep its license as an admitted insurer. As noted earlier, the financial requirements vary widely among the states.

Review of Annual Financial Statements. Insurers are required to submit annual financial statements to state insurance departments. The financial data must be submitted in a prescribed format, the NAIC Annual Statement, that provides detailed information on premiums written, expenses, investments, losses, reserves, and other financial information. The financial statements are analyzed to assess the insurer's financial position.

IRIS. The *Insurance Regulatory Information System* (IRIS) is used to detect insurers with potential solvency problems. This system is administered by the NAIC. Diagnostic tests are applied to the data submitted by insurers to provide early detection of insurers that may require closer monitoring.

IRIS has two phases. First, financial ratios and other reports are computed based on Annual Statement data. The reports are distributed to state insurance departments for review. Eleven ratios are computed, and insurers that do not meet certain criteria in four or more of the ratios are designated for additional review. Second, the financial ratios and selected Annual Statement data are then analyzed by a team of experienced state examiners and financial analysts. Based on these reviews, certain insurers may be designated for immediate attention or targeted regulatory attention. Insurers designated for immediate attention must be investigated by regulatory officials in the state where the insurer is domiciled. However, insurers designated for targeted attention are examined on a priority basis. Though helpful in setting regulatory priorities, IRIS has limitations as an early detection tool.

Onsite Field Examinations. Onsite field examinations are used to monitor the financial strength of insurers. State laws usually require that insurers be examined at least once every three to five years. By dividing the country into four geographical zones to avoid duplicate examination of multi-state insurers, the NAIC coordinates the field examinations of insurers that write business in several states.

Trends in Insurer Insolvency. Although the total remains relatively small, insurer insolvencies have increased in recent years. From 1981 through 1989, 184 life and property-casualty insurers failed.[8]

Slightly more than half of the insolvencies occurred during the three-year period from 1987 through 1989. The number of insurer insolvencies is relatively small when compared with the total number of insurers doing business in the United States. In mid-1990, 3,900 property and casualty insurers were doing business in the United States.[9] An estimated 2,350 U.S. life insurers were doing business at the end of 1989.[10] However, in 1989, only forty-four insurers became insolvent,[11] or less than one-half of one percent of the total number of insurers doing business.

However, there is some cause for concern over the effectiveness of solvency regulation and the financial safety of property and liability insurers, since the number of problem insurers has increased significantly in recent years. The number of property and liability insurers designated by the NAIC for closer state regulatory attention increased from 205 in the year 1983 to 622 in 1989, a sharp increase of 203 percent.[12]

Liquidation of Insolvent Insurers. If an insurer is technically insolvent, it is placed in receivership by the state insurance department. With proper management, successful rehabilitation may be possible. If the insurer cannot be rehabilitated, it is liquidated according to the state's insurance code. Many states now liquidate insolvent insurers according to the Uniform Insurers Liquidation Act drafted by the NAIC. The model act is designed to achieve uniformity in the liquidation of assets and payment of claims of a failed insurer. Under this act, creditors in each state where the insolvent insurer has conducted business are treated equally—creditors in the state where the insurer is domiciled do not receive preferential treatment.

Depending on state law, a priority system may be used to dispose of the failed insurer's assets. For example, in Nebraska, the administrative costs of liquidation are paid first; payment of unpaid claims and unearned premiums has second priority, followed next by general creditors, and finally by stockholders and surplus noteholders. Stockholders generally lose all or a large part of their original investment. If the insurer's assets are insufficient for paying all claims, the unpaid claims are submitted to the state guaranty fund for payment.

State Guaranty Funds. All states have property and liability insurance guaranty funds that provide for the payment of unpaid claims of insolvent insurers licensed in the particular state. With the exception of New York, the *assessment method* is used to raise the necessary funds to pay claims. Companies doing business in the state are assessed their share of unpaid claims. From 1969 through 1989, state guaranty fund net assessments on behalf of insolvent insurers totaled about $3.4 billion.[13] Insurers can recoup all or part of the assessments by rate increases, by special premium tax credits, and by refunds from the state guaranty fund.

New York does not use the assessment method. New York instead has a permanent preassessment solvency fund that assesses property and liability insurers on an ongoing basis. Insurers pay an amount equal to a certain percentage of their net direct premiums written, such as one-half of one percent until a specified amount has been reached. The funds are supposed to be kept in reserve until needed.

The characteristics of state guaranty funds vary by state. However, the following characteristics are common to all funds.[14]

1. *Assessments are made only when an insurer fails.* As indicated earlier, New York is the exception. The definition of "failure" varies among the states. Some states regard an insolvency order from a state court as evidence of failure. Others require a liquidation order from the state. All states have limits on the amounts insurers can be assessed in one year.

2. *All policies usually terminate within thirty days after the failure date.* Unpaid claims before termination, however, are still valid and will be paid out of the guaranty fund of the policyholder's state of residence if the insolvent insurer is licensed in the state. Under the NAIC's model act, if the failed insurer is not licensed in the state, a policyholder or claimant cannot file a claim with the guaranty fund but must seek payment by filing a claim against the failed insurer's assets, which are handled by the liquidator.[15]

3. *Claim coverage varies among the states.* No state fund covers reinsurance or surplus lines insurance (except New Jersey).

4. *There are maximum limits on allowed claims.* The maximum limit is usually the lesser of $300,000 or the policy limit. Some states have limits under $300,000, and a small number of states have much higher limits, such as $500,000 or $1 million.

5. *Most states provide for a refund of unearned premiums.* However, a few states have no unearned premium claim provision. In these states a policyholder in a failed company is not entitled to a refund of the unearned premium.

6. *A $100 deductible applies to unpaid claims in most states.* Many states exempt workers compensation claims from a deductible.

7. *The majority of states divide their guaranty funds into separate accounts,* usually auto, workers compensation, and other lines. Thus, auto or workers compensation assessments can be limited to insurers that write only that type of insurance.

8. *Recovery of assessments varies among the states.* Thirty-two

states permit insurers to recover assessments by a rate increase. The remaining states generally allow insurers to reduce their annual state premium taxes, usually over a period of five years. As a result, taxpayers and the general public, as well as insureds, are subsidizing the unpaid claims of insolvent insurers.

Because of the increase in insurer insolvencies in recent years, state guaranty funds in certain states have been under heavy financial strain. Policyholders of failed insurers often must wait a long time before their claims are paid. Because insurers are assessed for unpaid claims only after the state insurance department orders an insolvent insurer to be liquidated, the result often is considerable delay in the payment of claims.

As noted earlier, the maximum amount payable on a claim varies among the states. Depending on the state, a large commercial insured can have a substantial unpaid loss. Consider, for example, an unpaid burglary claim in the amount of $500,000. The entire claim would be paid in Rhode Island, but only sixty percent ($300,000) in Nebraska, and only ten percent ($50,000) in Colorado.

Reasons for Insolvency. The Subcommittee on Oversight and Investigation in the U.S. House of Representatives investigated the failure of more than 150 property and liability insurers since 1969. The subcommittee examined in considerable detail the failures of Mission Insurance Company, Integrity Insurance Company, Transit Casualty, and the Anglo-American Insurance Company. These four failures alone were estimated to have cost the American public more than $5 billion.[16] The subcommittee also studied the near failures of Ohio Indemnity Company and the Insurance Company of Ireland.

The major causes of insolvency are summarized as follows:[17]

1. *Inadequate rates.* Some failed insurers had cut rates excessively to increase market share. Substantial losses resulted from the underpriced business and poor investment returns. Loss reserves also were inadequate.

2. *Excessive delegation of management authority.* Insurance managers in the failed companies relied excessively on the judgment of managing general agents, brokers, and other insurers, which often resulted in a financial conflict of interest. In particular, a managing general agent (MGA) was often granted excessive authority. A managing general agent has the authority to underwrite new business, bind the insurer, handle claims, and even arrange reinsurance. To earn commissions, a managing general agent may write low quality business that later results in substantial underwriting losses.

3. *Holding companies.* Another reason for failure is that some insurers became too overleveraged, and liquid assets were drained off by affiliated companies. Affiliated companies sometimes are used as dodges to confuse and evade the scrutiny of regulators.

4. *Refusal of reinsurers to pay claims.* Some companies failed because reinsurers refused to pay their share of claims. The subcommittee concluded that in the case of Mission, Integrity, and Transit, the reinsurance system broke down entirely. These primary insurers had attempted to transfer most of the risk on unprofitable business to hundreds of reinsurers around the world. Reinsurers subsequently refused to pay their share of mounting underwriting losses because of alleged fraud and misrepresentation by the ceding insurers.[18]

5. *Unreliable solvency information.* Another criticism of solvency regulation is that much of the information used to measure solvency is unreliable. The financial information submitted by insurers was not verified by independent auditors or actuaries. Loss reserve data can be particularly misleading.

6. *Inadequate regulation.* The subcommittee also concluded that solvency regulation suffers because of inadequate financial resources, lack of coordination, infrequent regulatory examinations, poor information and communications, and uneven implementation. Insurance licenses often are granted to seriously undercapitalized companies. Background checks on the honesty of the management of newly formed insurance companies often are inadequate. Instead of demanding the highest financial and character qualifications, some regulators are extremely reluctant to deny granting, or to withdraw, a license unless there is a clear legal record of fraud. Moreover, criminal prosecution of dishonest executives is hampered because of limited resources, limited penalties, jurisdictional problems, and a reluctance to prosecute dishonest wrongdoers.

Challenges in Solvency Regulation. Solvency regulation presents some significant challenges. Among them are the time lag in obtaining data, inadequate resources, underqualified personnel, and inadequate sharing of information.[19]

Time Lag in Determining Problem Insurers. Annual Statements are submitted two months after the end of the accounting year, and they can take as long as three months to review. *This time lag delays detection of a problem and allows insolvent and struggling insurers to continue operating for months.* Moreover, most states require field examinations only once every three to five years, and the examinations often take months or years to complete. Meanwhile, problem insurers continue to operate and write new business.

Inadequate Resources. Some state insurance departments are understaffed and have insufficient financial resources to monitor the solvency of insurers in an effective manner. The GAO found that in the five states visited in its study on solvency regulation, twenty-six examiners were required to manually review 6,450 annual statements, or one reviewer for each 248 annual statements.[20]

Lack of Professional Qualifications for Field Examiners. Another defect is that some field examiners do not meet NAIC qualification standards for examiners who participate in zone examinations. The NAIC prescribes that every zone examiner be certified by the National Society of Financial Examiners as an Accredited Financial Examiner (AFE) and that the examiner-in-charge be a Certified Financial Examiner (CFE). However, many states employ examiners underqualified by NAIC standards.[21]

Inadequate Sharing of Information by the States. States vary in the amount of information about problem insurers that will be shared with other states. Some states openly share all information with other states. However, other states are reluctant to share information on problem insurers with other states even though the interstate operations of many large insurers and state responsibility under a guaranty fund make interstate sharing of solvency information absolutely necessary.

Regulators, insurance company officials, and the NAIC have made several worthwhile suggestions to improve solvency regulation:

- *Certification of insurance departments.* The NAIC has approved a plan to certify state insurance departments that meet certain minimum standards. The standards include CPA audits, actuarial opinions on reserve adequacy, timely field exams, and much more.
- *Monitoring of reinsurers.* Annual statements could be required to contain more accurate and complete information on reinsurance transactions. The NAIC is also developing a new computer-based reporting system to detect potential reinsurance problems before a reinsurer becomes insolvent.
- *Federal guaranty fund.* A federal guaranty fund could be created to pay claims of insolvent insurers.

Rate Regulation

Rate regulation is another important regulatory area. This section discusses the objectives of rate regulation, the different types of rating laws, the arguments for prior approval and open competition rating laws, and trends in rate regulation.

Objectives of Rate Regulation. Rate regulation is designed both to maintain insurer solvency and to protect policyholders. The major objectives of rate regulation are to ensure that rates are adequate, not excessive, and not unfairly discriminatory.

Adequate. Premiums for a specific line of insurance should be high enough to pay all claims and expenses related to those premiums. The purpose of this requirement is to maintain insurer solvency. If rates are inadequate, an insurer might fail, and policyholders and third-party claimants would be financially harmed if their claims were not paid. The objective of rate adequacy is complicated by the fact that an insurer usually does not know what its actual costs will be when the policy is sold. Premiums are paid in advance, but they might not be sufficient to pay all related claims and expenses that occur later. An unexpected increase in the number of claims or the amounts paid can make the premium inadequate.

Many factors can complicate the regulatory objective of adequate rates:

- Insurers might charge inadequate rates in response to keen price competition since otherwise they would lose business.
- State rate approval systems might not approve insurers' requests for adequate rates for political reasons or because of disagreement over the level of requested rates.
- Unanticipated events might lead to higher losses than projected when rates were set.

Although rate adequacy is a goal of insurance regulation, no method of rate regulation guarantees that rates are adequate.

Not Excessive. A second regulatory objective is that rates should not be excessive. In other words, insurers should not earn excessive or unreasonable profits. Regulators have considerable latitude and discretion in determining whether rates are excessive for a given line of insurance, and they consider numerous factors. These factors include (1) the number of insurers selling a specific coverage in the rating territory, (2) the relative market share of competing insurers, (3) the degree of price variation among the competing insurers, (4) past and prospective loss experience for a given line of insurance, (5) presence of catastrophe hazards, (6) margin for underwriting profit and contingencies, (7) marketing expenses for a given line of insurance, and (8) special judgment factors that may apply to a given line.[22]

Recently, regulators have used the *fair rate of return* concept in determining whether an insurer's rates are adequate or excessive. An insurer should expect at least some minimum rate of return on the equity invested in its insurance operations. An insurer's fair rate of return presumably should resemble the rate of return applicable to other types of businesses, especially if insurers are to attract investment capital. In fact, insurers argue that theirs is a business involving a higher degree of risk than many and that higher risks generally should be accompanied by higher returns. To date, there has been little agreement as to what constitutes a fair rate of return for insurers.

Not Unfairly Discriminatory. The word "discrimination," as it usually is used, carries negative connotations, but the word itself is neutral, implying only the ability to differentiate among things. Discrimination, in the neutral sense, is the key to insurance rating. However, the discrimination done must be fair and consistent. *This means that loss exposures that are roughly similar with respect to expected losses and expenses should not be charged substantially different rates.* For example, two women age twenty-five in good health who buy the same type and amount of life insurance from the same insurer should not be charged different rates.

It is important to note that only unfair rate discrimination is prohibited, not fair discrimination. If loss exposures are substantially different in terms of expected losses and expenses, then different rates can be charged. For example, if two women age twenty-five and sixty-five are in good health and purchase the same type and amount of life insurance from the same insurer, it is not unfair rate discrimination to charge the older woman a higher rate. The higher probability of death for a woman age sixty-five clearly and fairly justifies a higher rate.

Types of Rating Laws. The rates that property and liability underwriters can charge in any state are affected by that state's rating laws. In general, the major types of state rating laws are as follows:

- Mandatory state or bureau rates
- Prior approval laws
- File-and-use laws
- Flex rating laws
- Open competition laws

These laws apply not only to rates for a new line of insurance, but also to rate changes.

Mandatory Rates. Under a mandatory rate law, rates are set by some state agency or rating bureau, and all licensed insurers are required to use those rates.

Prior Approval Laws. Under a prior approval law, rates used must be approved by the state insurance department before they can be used. Prior approval laws have been criticized by insurers because there is often considerable delay in obtaining a rate increase. As a result, a rate increase may be inadequate by the time it is approved. Furthermore, the statistical data required by the state insurance department may not readily be available.

File-and-Use Laws. Under a file-and-use law, rates have to be filed with the state insurance department, but they can then be used immediately. The state insurance department has the authority to disapprove the rates if they cannot be justified or if they violate state law. A file-and-use law overcomes the problems of delay associated with prior approval laws.

A variation of file and use is a *use-and-file law* that allows insurers to put rate changes into effect and later submit filing information that is subject to review by regulatory officials.

Flex Rating Laws. Some states have enacted an innovative rating law called "flex rating." Under a flex rating law, prior approval is required only if the new rates exceed a certain percentage above (and sometimes below) the rates previously filed. Insurers are permitted to increase or reduce their rates within the established band or range without prior approval. Typically, margins of five or ten percent are permitted. Flex rating permits insurers to make rate adjustments quickly in response to changing market conditions and loss experience, but it dampens wide swings within a short period of time. Flex rating also may restrict insurers from drastically reducing premiums to increase market share. The result should be smoother insurance pricing cycles.

Open Competition Laws. Under an open competition law (also called a no-filing law), rates do not have to be filed with the state insurance department. Market prices based on competition, rather than the discretionary acts of regulators, determine the price and availability of insurance. However, insurers may be required to furnish rate schedules and supporting statistical data to regulatory officials, and the state insurance department has the authority to monitor competition and disapprove rates if necessary. The standards of adequate, nonexcessive, and equitable rates still apply.

Is Strict Rate Regulation Desirable? There is a conflict between the groups that support prior approval laws and strict rate regulation, and groups that promote open competition laws and free markets. In general, consumer groups and politicians tend to support prior approval or other forms of strict regulation, while insurers and economists tend to support open competition.

Groups supporting prior approval laws offer the following arguments in support of their position:

- Insurers must justify their requests for rate increases with supporting actuarial data.
- Prior approval laws tend to maintain insurer solvency. Since regulators review rate data, rates can be set at adequate levels so that insurer solvency is maintained.
- Prior approval laws keep rates reasonable and prevent insurers from charging excessive rates. There is a widely held view that auto insurers are earning excessive profits and that rates can be reduced only by direct government action.

Those supporting open competition laws advance the following arguments:

- In prior approval states, rate increases may be inadequate for writing profitable business. Inadequate rates may force insurers to reduce the amount of new business written or may even force them to withdraw from the market. Thus, insurers may respond by not writing new business or by withdrawing from a territory, which may lead to an availability problem.
- Prior approval laws may distort incentives for controlling claim costs. This argument is applied largely to auto insurance. To make auto insurance more affordable, regulators may reduce rates for drivers who face the highest premiums by increasing rates for other drivers. This can be done by limiting the rates insurers can charge motorists who are in a residual market plan or by restricting the use of age, sex, or territory as ratemaking variables. The result is that high-risk drivers are more likely to drive; they are more likely to purchase expensive cars; and they are less likely to exercise caution in preventing accidents and theft losses than if their rates were not subsidized.[23]
- Prior approval laws may result in an increase in the residual markets. Residual market plans are special government-sponsored plans that make automobile insurance available to motorists who are unable to obtain coverage in the standard markets. There is considerable evidence that in states with strict rate suppression, the proportion of drivers in residual market plans is much higher than in states with competitive rating laws. Under open competition, the equilibrium market price is determined by market forces, not by government regulators. As a result, most motorists can be insured in the voluntary standard market by paying market prices.
- Open competition laws are less expensive to administer. Regulators are not required to review thousands of rate filings or hold costly hearings. As a result, limited regulatory resources can be

devoted to higher priority areas, such as solvency regulation and consumer affairs.

- Open competition laws tend to overcome the limitations of prior approval laws. Under an open competition law, rates can be adjusted more quickly in response to changing economic and market conditions. Fewer political pressures are encountered, and the need for supporting actuarial data is reduced.
- Price competition among insurers will keep rates reasonable and equitable. Free market forces rather than artificial government intervention will curtail excessive rates.

More than 100 research studies have been published concerning the financial and economic effects of insurance rate regulation. A large number of studies compared pricing and underwriting results between states with regulated rates and states with unregulated rates. Statewide loss ratios (defined as ratio of incurred losses to earned premiums for direct business) were commonly used to compare these results. In general, the higher the loss ratio, the lower the unit price of insurance (ratio of premiums to losses). A number of recently published studies showed that states with regulated auto insurance rates had higher loss ratios (lower unit prices) than did states with competitive pricing.

Three broad conclusions emerge from an analysis of these empirical studies on the impact of rate regulation on auto insurance prices.[24]

- *Recently published studies suggest that rate regulation helps to keep auto insurance premiums down relative to loss costs.* As noted earlier, rate regulation tends to increase loss ratios and lower unit prices. Regulators may hold down rates to make auto insurance more affordable.
- *Tight rate regulation that keeps auto insurance rates down and below free market levels may lead to an increase in residual market volume.* Thus, regulated auto insurance rates that are below free market levels are not a blessing to all drivers. Insurers respond to the lower rates by reducing the quality of services provided or by reducing the amount of auto insurance written, and they ration the available insurance to the best drivers. With inadequate voluntary market rates, a higher proportion of drivers are placed in a residual market plan such as an auto insurance plan ("assigned risk plan").
- *In highly regulated states in which rates are inadequate, insurers will withdraw from the market entirely.* For example, because of inadequate rates, twenty-seven insurers withdrew from the personal lines market in South Carolina in 1990. In other states as well, several major insurers have cut back on

their auto insurance operations or withdrawn from the market entirely.[25]

- *Peer review by insurers.* Insurers would be encouraged to "blow the whistle" on other insurers that are engaging in excessive price cutting, fraudulent or questionable activities, or other activities that could result in insolvency. Under such a system, insurers would recommend to regulators that a potential insolvency problem should be investigated. This recommendation is based on the belief that the industry will be more aware of a company's financial problems long before the examination process confirms that a problem exists. Also, all insurers face guaranty fund assessments whenever another company fails.

- *Limitations on junk bonds.* Some states have passed legislation that limits the percentage of assets that can be invested in junk bonds. Junk bonds are high-yielding bonds below investment grade in which the probability of default is relatively high, especially during business recessions. In the past, some insurers, primarily life insurers, have invested heavily in junk bonds. Such insurers are more vulnerable to financial problems if a large percentage of the junk bonds are in default. By restricting junk bonds to a small percentage of assets, solvency problems from this source are reduced.

Contract Regulation

Insurance contracts present another important area of regulation.[26] Regulation of insurance contracts is necessary for the following reasons:

- *Insurance contracts are complex documents.* Most insurance contracts are difficult to interpret and understand. Thus, regulation of their structure and content is necessary.
- *Insurance contracts are almost always drafted by insurers who sell the contracts to the public on a take-it-or-leave-it basis.* Since insurers could draft contracts that are narrow, restrictive, or deceptive, regulation is needed to protect policyholders.
- *If a covered loss occurs, it is important both to society and to the insured that insurers fulfill their contractual obligations.* Regulation of insurance contracts helps to achieve this end.

Insurance contracts are regulated by three principal means: (1) legislation, (2) administrative rules and regulations, and (3) the courts.

Legislation. Regulation of insurance contracts starts with the legislature, which can regulate the nature and content of insurance coverages sold in a state. Legislative contract regulation may take one of four approaches: standard forms, mandatory provisions, forms approval, or readability standards.

Standard Forms. The law may require that a standard policy be used in the state to insure property or liability loss exposures. A standard policy is an identical policy that all insurers must use if the policy is sold in the state. For many years, most states required use of the Standard Fire Policy as the basic document to insure fixed-local property against the peril of fire.

Another example of a standard contract is the automobile insurance contract used in Massachusetts. The legislature has prescribed the wording of compulsory motor vehicle insurance contracts sold in the state.

Mandatory Provisions. Legislation can instead require that certain standard mandatory contractual provisions appear in certain types of insurance contracts. For example, the states require that certain contractual provisions must appear in all individual health insurance contracts, while other provisions are optional. The required and optional provisions are based on a model bill developed by the NAIC. There are twenty-three standard and uniform health insurance policy provisions. Twelve provisions are required; the remainder are optional. Moreover, the states require that workers compensation insurance, no-fault auto coverage, and often uninsured motorists coverage contain certain contractual provisions.

State regulations may require that the required policy provisions meet certain minimum standards, providing at least a minimum level of protection.

Forms Approval. Legislation may require that policy forms be filed and approved by the state. Among other things, it is believed that such approval helps protect policyholders against ambiguous, misleading, or deceptive contracts. Many states require that a policy form be submitted for approval before it may be used. However, if a specified period elapses and the contract has not been *disapproved*, the contract is "deemed" to have been approved. (Some states permit the state insurance department to extend the review period.) The purpose of this "deemer provision" in state regulatory statutes is to encourage a prompt review of the form, but it can cause the review to be perfunctory.

Some states have a *file-and-use* law that permits insurers to use a new form immediately, subject to subsequent disapproval by the insurance department.

Readability Standards. Legislation may require that insurance contracts be readable. The law may specify that the policy must meet a certain test of readability. The law also can specify the style and form of the contract as well as the size of print. Such readability legislation has influenced the drafting of homeowners and auto insurance contracts, but readability tests do not necessarily measure understandability.

Advantages and Disadvantages of Policy Standardization. Advisory organizations such as Insurance Services Office (ISO) and American Association of Insurance Services (AAIS) draft standard contracts and endorsements that participating insurance companies may use. For example, the various homeowners forms, personal auto policy, and commercial property and liability forms drafted by ISO are widely used by its participating companies throughout the United States.

Standard insurance contracts and uniform policy provisions provide some advantages to both insureds and insurers, including the following:

● Consumers do not have to compare differences in policy provisions and language among different insurers when all use the same contract.

● Courts can interpret the contractual provisions and coverages more consistently when standard contracts and provisions are used. There are fewer conflicting court decisions.

● Since standard contracts are being sold, insurers can use comparable loss data and pooled experience for ratemaking purposes.

● Standard contracts are especially important for smaller insurers who might have insufficient actuarial data to produce accurate rates based on loss experience involving their own policy forms.

● When losses involve two or more insurers, claim settlement problems are reduced if the policies contain uniform provisions.

● State insurance departments might find it difficult to review the policy provisions carefully if each insurer drafted its own form.

● Standard contracts reduce the possibility that insurers will draft contracts that are ambiguous, unduly restrictive, and misleading to insureds.

Standard contracts and provisions have certain disadvantages, including the following:

● A standard contract might not meet the special needs of insureds who require tailored coverages.

● Standard contracts might reduce the freedom, desire, and flexibility of insurers to innovate and develop new coverages.

● Policyholders must purchase and pay for the entire contract, which might contain certain coverages the insured does not need or desire.

● A legislatively prescribed statutory contract is difficult to change. A legislature could be convinced that change is necessary and desirable but, because of other demands, may leave the policy unchanged for long periods of time.

Administrative Rules, Regulations, and Guidelines. Administrative rules, regulations, and guidelines are the second method for regulating insurance contracts. These may be stated in (1) regulations communicated by the state insurance department to insurers, (2) informal circulars or bulletins from the same source, and (3) precedents set in the approval process. State insurance departments carry out specific directives from the legislature, or the departments implement the general authority they have to regulate insurance contracts. For example, the state insurance department may require that certain language and wording appear in certain policy provisions or make it known to insurers that certain types of policy provisions will be disapproved.

Courts. The courts are called on to determine whether insurance laws concerning contracts are constitutional and whether administrative rulings and regulations are legal and consistent with state law. The courts are also important in interpreting ambiguous and confusing policy provisions, in determining whether certain losses are covered under the contract, and in resolving other disputes between insurers and policyholders over contract coverages and provisions.

Adverse court decisions often prompt redrafting of specific policy language and contractual provisions. For example, based on the legal doctrine of concurrent causation, certain courts ruled that if a loss under an "all-risks" policy is due to two perils, of which one is excluded and the other is not, the entire loss is covered. As a result of this doctrine, insurers found that they were required to pay certain flood and earthquake claims they had believed were excluded by their homeowners policies. Subsequent revision of the language in many "all-risks" property policies explicitly excluded coverage for flood and earthquake losses in cases where another unexcluded peril contributed in causing the loss.

Market Conduct Surveillance

During the last several years, the Market Conduct Surveillance Task Force of the National Association of Insurance Commissioners has initiated several improvements in the market conduct examination process. The *Market Conduct Examiners Handbook* provides better guidance for examiners in conducting market conduct examinations. Information on completed examinations is forwarded directly to the NAIC office and disseminated to all states so that current reports from other states can be utilized whenever possible in lieu of an additional examination.

Among the most important market conduct concerns for regulators are claims practices and consumer protection.

Claims Practices. All states have laws that prohibit certain claims practices. *Unfair claims practices laws* prohibit a wide variety of unethical and illegal claims practices. The laws generally are patterned after the NAIC Model Unfair Claim Settlement Practices Act. Prohibited insurer practices typically include the following:

- Misrepresenting important facts or policy provisions relating to the coverage at issue
- Not attempting in good faith to pay claims where liability is reasonably clear
- Attempting to settle a claim for less than the amount that a reasonable person believes he or she is entitled to receive based on advertising material that accompanies or is made part of the application
- Failing to approve or deny coverage of a claim within a reasonable period after a proof-of-loss statement has been completed

Without strict regulatory controls on claims practices, the fundamental social and contractual purpose of protecting policyholders is sometimes defeated. In addition, unfair claims practices tarnish the offending insurer's image and reputation; public confidence in the insurance industry is reduced; and insurers appear to hide behind the "fine print" of contractual provisions to deny claims to the policyholders' detriment. Fair and equitable claim payments require honesty and fairness on both sides. Fair claim payments also mean that the payment of fraudulent claims submitted by dishonest insureds should be vigorously resisted, and that excessive claim settlements should be avoided. Valid and legitimate claims, however, should be paid promptly and fairly with a minimum of legal formality.

Consumer Protection. State insurance departments generally lack direct authority to order insurers to pay disputed claims when factual questions are at issue. However, most state insurance departments investigate and follow up every consumer complaint, at least to the extent of getting a response from the insurer involved. Most consumer complaints are presumed to have some basis, and the majority of them are resolved in favor of the consumer. Although many states compute complaint ratios (ratios of complaints to premium volume), few states publicize the ratios or make them widely available to consumers.[27] This information may be especially relevant with disputed auto insurance claims, where certain insurers have consistently higher complaint ratios than others.

To make consumers more knowledgeable about the cost of insurance, some states publish shoppers' guides and other forms of consumer information. The guides typically provide cost data on life insurance, auto insurance, and homeowners insurance.

Federal Regulation of Insurance

As a result of the McCarran-Ferguson Act, state regulation dominates the government regulation of insurance. Nevertheless, a number of federal laws have a significant regulatory impact on various aspects of insurer operations and activities. A few of them are discussed here.

Federal Antitrust Laws. The Sherman Antitrust Act prohibits contracts, combination, or conspiracy in restraint of trade and monopolies that restrain trade. However, because of McCarran-Ferguson, federal antitrust laws apply to insurance only to the extent that the industry is not regulated by state law. Thus, federal antitrust laws generally do not apply to insurance, but the exemption is not absolute. The Sherman Act also forbids firms from engaging in any acts or agreements to boycott, coerce, or intimidate; insurers remain subject to federal law in these areas.

Employee Retirement Income Security Act of 1974. The Employee Retirement Income Security Act (ERISA) was passed by Congress to protect the interests of participants in employee benefit plans, as well as the interests of their beneficiaries. ERISA's complex requirements, in many ways, directly affect the design of insurance products that must comply with ERISA. For example, private pension plans subject to the act must meet certain minimum funding standards. Minimum vesting standards must be followed (vesting is the right of the employee to the employer's contributions even though the employee terminates service before retirement). Certain fiduciary standards must be met; disclosure statements and information must be furnished to employees; certain transactions are prohibited; and certain investment practices must be followed, in addition to numerous additional regulations. ERISA is administered by the Department of Labor and the Treasury Department.

Especially significant is the fact that ERISA supersedes state laws, other than insurance regulatory laws, that relate to employee benefit plans. However, recent court cases have affirmed that this exemption does not apply to self-funded employee benefit plans, which are thus regulated by ERISA rather than by the states.

Securities and Exchange Commission (SEC). Like other publicly held corporations, an insurance company whose stock is publicly traded must comply with the disclosure requirements of the federal securities laws. Responsibility for enforcing these laws rests with the Securities and Exchange Commission.

While the financial statements filed with state insurance regulators must meet the states' statutory accounting requirements, financial statements filed with the SEC must be in accordance with the Generally

Accepted Accounting Principles (GAAP) standards applicable to corporations in general.

In addition to accounting requirements, the SEC has responsibility for the regulation of variable life insurance and variable annuities, products sold by life insurers. Because variable annuities, in some ways, resemble mutual funds, a 1959 Supreme Court decision[28] held that variable annuities should be subject to many of the same federal laws and regulations as mutual funds. Life insurance agents who wish to sell variable annuities must be licensed by the SEC; a state life insurance agent's license does not grant authority to sell variable annuities.

Internal Revenue Code. Like most other business corporations, insurance companies are subject to federal taxation in accordance with the Internal Revenue Code (IRC). Basically, insurance companies are taxed like other corporations. However, special sections of the IRC deal specifically with insurer operations and supersede certain portions of the general tax law, giving recognition to the unique characteristics of insurance companies. Special treatment is given to the calculation of underwriting income, which is determined as the difference between premiums earned on insurance contracts during the tax year and losses and expenses incurred, an approach that parallels statutory rather than GAAP accounting. Other IRC provisions apply to methods for ascertaining the reasonableness of estimated loss reserves and to the ways in which investment income and capital gains and losses are calculated. The ways in which insurers' results are tabulated for tax purposes can have a profound effect on their tax liabilities.

Other Federal Actions Affecting Insurers. The federal government continues to have an important regulatory impact on the insurance industry, as illustrated by the following property-liability-related examples:

- Motor truck cargo carriers must carry compulsory liability insurance purchased from private insurers. The amount of required insurance depends on type of carrier and the goods carried. For nonhazardous goods such as meat or produce, at least $750,000 of liability insurance must be carried by for-hire carriers. For hazardous materials such as gasoline or explosives, substantially higher limits are required.
- The Environmental Protection Agency (EPA) requires firms with underground storage tanks to meet certain financial responsibility rules. The EPA guidelines for insurance require firms to carry a certain amount of third-party liability insurance and coverage for on-site and off-site cleanup. The financial responsibility requirements vary depending on the situation. For example, if the tanks are used in petroleum production, refining, or

marketing, the firm must carry at least $1 million of liability coverage for each occurrence. An annual aggregate limit is also required.

- Firms that bid on government contracts may be required to furnish surety bonds and to carry certain kinds of insurance.

Many more examples could be given, but the point has been made. The federal government currently has an important regulatory influence on private insurers even though the business of insurance is regulated primarily by the states.

THE GOVERNMENT AS INSURER

In addition to its role as regulator, government can also influence the insurance business through direct intervention. By competing with, reinsuring, or perhaps supplanting private insurance companies, government can significantly alter the price and availability of insurance. Private insurance is generally preferred, but various reasons have justified government insurance in certain cases. Government insurance programs include social programs, certain types of otherwise unavailable property-liability insurance, and financial security programs.

The Roles of Government Insurers

The government may be an exclusive insurer, it may work in partnership with private insurers, or it may be a competitor of private insurers.

Exclusive Insurer. The government may be an exclusive insurer either because the law grants exclusive status or because no private insurer offers a competing plan. Governmental insurers may function either as primary insurers or as reinsurers.

- *Primary insurer.* A federal or state government can function as a primary insurer by providing the coverage and paying all claims and expenses.
- *Reinsurer.* The government can function as a reinsurer either by providing 100 percent reinsurance to private insurers writing a particular coverage or by reinsuring on an excess basis.

Partnership With Private Insurers. Government may offer a plan as a partner with private insurers. The partnerships may vary considerably. One type of partnership exists when the government operates a reinsurance plan, such as for crop insurance, providing reinsurance on specific loss exposures in which private insurers retain only part of the loss. In other cases, such as the federal flood insurance program, the federal government bears the risk of loss, but policies are delivered through private insurers and insurance producers.

Competition With Private Insurers. Government may operate an insurance plan in direct competition with private insurers. When this is done, government employees perform essentially the same marketing, underwriting, actuarial, and claims functions as a private insurance company.

Reasons for Government Insurance

The following basic reasons are among those used to rationalize and justify government participation in insurance:

1. To fill insurance needs not met by private insurers
2. To force people to buy a particular type of insurance
3. To provide convenience to insurance purchasers
4. To obtain greater efficiency
5. To achieve collateral social purposes[29]

Unmet Needs. Government participation in the insurance business has been defended partially on the grounds that private insurers have been unable or unwilling to satisfy certain needs for insurance and therefore that public insurers must do so in order to meet legitimate public demands. This void exists because some exposures fail to possess the ideal characteristics of a commercially insurable exposure.

Compulsion. Most government programs are deemed to need the element of compulsion for success. For example, some employers would not purchase workers compensation insurance if they were not, in effect, required to. Similarly, the general population might not save enough money for contingencies such as old age dependency.

If it is deemed necessary that a given insurance program be compulsory, several reasons have been given as to why it might also be necessary that the government do the insuring:

- Many observers believe that a government insurer is a practical necessity in the operation of any large, compulsory insurance system such as the Old Age, Survivors, Disability and Health Insurance (OASDHI) program. The large size, complexity, and necessity for constant adjustments in the program are thought to make government insuring activities essential. Each session of Congress considers some changes in the program. Use of private intermediaries to translate the changing law into administrative procedures might prove extremely cumbersome.
- Tax collections to finance OASDHI or any other large compul-

sory national program can be effected through the Internal Revenue Service.

- Many argue that it is unwise to allow private insurers to earn profits from a publicly mandated program.

Convenience. It often seems easier and faster for legislative bodies to establish an insurance fund for some particular purpose than to attempt to publicize the "need" among private insurers, invite and analyze bids, and supervise and regulate the resulting plans. Moreover, private insurers would not seem likely to respond adequately to some insurance needs.

Speed was an important consideration when the federal government established war risk insurance during World War II. Additionally, it was not clear whether the private insurance industry would have been able to handle the exposure adequately.

With respect to flood insurance, only the federal government seemed to have the ability to coordinate not only insurance, but also flood plain surveys, land use control, and integration of flood insurance benefits with disaster relief administered by the Federal Emergency Management Agency.

Efficiency. Efficiency, or the saving of taxpayers' funds, appears to be a major, but often unspoken, rationale in government participation in insurance. When coverage is compulsory, no need seems to exist to pay for selling effort or to pay salaries or sales commissions. Private insurers use sales personnel to market the coverages they sell, and it is not practical to consider the elimination of commissions to insurance sales representatives. Governments avoid these sales costs by setting up their own insuring channels.

Collateral Social Purpose. Government participation in insurance often is justified for societal purposes other than insurance. For example, workers compensation laws have the important side purposes of encouraging injury prevention and rehabilitating injured workers. Similarly, the National Flood Insurance Program provides strong incentives to amend and enforce building codes and otherwise reduce the exposure of floods in new construction.

Types of Government Insurance

While a diverse array of government insurance programs presently exists and new ones are always possible, most of them fall into three broad categories. Those categories are social insurance, property-liability coverages, and financial security programs. Examples of each illustrate the extent of government insurance in the United States.

Social Insurance. Social insurance plans are designed to solve various broad social problems. Certain conditions ordinarily characterize social insurance plans, such as the element of compulsion, absence of a "needs test," and a system of financing under which definite premiums are charged to members of the insured group or to their employers.

In social insurance, the loss need not be accidental, and the plan must be set up under "law." Most social insurance plans share a variety of characteristics:

1. They provide only a small benefit received not as charity but as a matter of right.
2. They provide benefits only loosely related to premiums paid so that low-income persons may receive a larger benefit relative to premiums paid than do high-income persons.
3. They provide an element of compulsion, including compulsory contributions by those who are not personally insured (for example, employers or the government).
4. They contain a large element of unpredictability of total cost (that is, benefits) with accompanying instability of premiums.
5. They are usually administered by monopolistic insurers (that is, the government).[30]

One of the major differences between private and public insurance is the matter of "equity versus adequacy." A major premise of private insurance is equity (that is, treating policyholders fairly by charging them premiums in direct proportion to the loss exposure borne or the benefits paid). By contrast, a major goal of social insurance is to meet the minimum level of adequacy in providing benefits to the public in response to some widespread or far-reaching hazard.[31]

Most social insurance plans require attachment to the labor force as a condition for coverage. This condition exists because most social insurance plans are aimed at restoring employment income when some peril such as unemployment, job injury, or old age interrupts this income. Most plans meeting the definition of social insurance do not benefit persons not normally working in the paid work force. Examples of such persons are housewives, children, students, or the permanently disabled. Unless they are covered as dependents of workers, they normally do not receive social insurance benefits. Other plans, such as public welfare, have been designed for these excluded groups.

To promote certain select social goals, the government may provide a subsidy in the form of favorable income tax treatment. For example, to encourage the growth of private pensions and other retirement plans, employer contributions into a qualified plan are income tax deductible, and the contributions are not taxed as income to covered employees until the funds are distributed. Likewise, to encourage the growth of private health insurance, employer contributions into a qualified group medical expense plan are also income tax deductible, and the contributions are not taxed as income to covered employees. The fact that group and mass merchandised property and liability insurance plans do not enjoy the same favorable income tax treatment has discouraged the growth of such plans.

Social Security. The United States government functions for the most part as a primary insurer in the social security program, which is designed primarily to promote social goals. The social security program is a massive public income maintenance program providing valuable protection to individuals and families against the financial consequences of the following:

- Premature death or disability of a wage earner
- Insufficient income during retirement
- Sizable medical expenses incurred by the aged and by certain groups under age sixty-five

More than nine out of ten workers are currently employed in occupations covered by social security, and roughly one in six Americans receives a monthly social security check. The program came into existence as a result of the Social Security Act of 1935, which instituted direct government intervention in the economy to deal with massive unemployment and widespread financial hardship as a result of the Great Depression of the 1930s.

The benefits, eligibility requirements, and other features of the social security program are examined in CPCU 2.

Unemployment Compensation. The objectives of unemployment compensation programs are (1) to provide weekly cash benefits for a short period to covered workers who are involuntarily unemployed for temporary periods, (2) to help unemployed workers find jobs, (3) to charge the costs of unemployment to firms responsible for the unemployment (accomplished through experience rating), and (4) to help stabilize the economy during periods of business recession.

All states have unemployment compensation programs that pay cash benefits to eligible would-be workers who are involuntarily unemployed. Weekly cash benefits equal to some fraction of the unemployed worker's previous earnings can be paid up to a certain maximum number of weeks. An extended-benefits program is available that pays additional benefits to workers who have exhausted their regular benefits in states with high unemployment.

Eligibility requirements for benefits are strict. Most jurisdictions require a one-week waiting period before benefits are payable. The unemployed worker also must earn qualifying wages during his or her base period, register for work at a local public employment office, be able and available to work, and actively seek work. In addition, the unemployed worker must not be disqualified from receiving benefits by actions such as quitting his or her job without good cause, being fired for misconduct, or refusing suitable work.

Unemployment is extremely difficult to insure privately. The loss exposures are not independent; the potential for a catastrophic loss is present; the unemployment rate is difficult to forecast accurately because of complex social and economic conditions and changing government policy; and government action is needed to increase unemployment insurance taxes to finance the programs during periods in which state unemployment reserve amounts are low or depleted.

Railroad Workers.   Railroad workers are covered under two separate social insurance programs: (1) the Railroad Retirement Act and (2) the Railroad Unemployment Insurance Act. The current Railroad Retirement Act provides monthly cash benefits to retired and disabled workers and their dependents, and survivor benefits to families of insured workers.

Unemployment insurance and sickness benefits are provided under the Railroad Unemployment Insurance Act. A separate unemployment insurance plan for railroad workers was established in 1938 because workers whose jobs required the crossing of state lines sometimes found they were not eligible for unemployment compensation benefits in any of the states in which they worked. The present program now pays benefits to unemployed workers for limited periods. Sickness benefits and special maternity benefits are also available.

Temporary Disability Insurance.   Some people believe that a social insurance program covering nonoccupational disabilities for a temporary period is justified because many workers are inadequately protected against the loss of wages during a period of short-term disability. Five states, Puerto Rico, and the railroad industry have temporary disability insurance laws (also called cash sickness insurance) that pay disability income benefits to covered workers who are temporarily disabled because of a *nonoccupational accident or sickness.*

Disabled workers must meet certain eligibility requirements to qualify for disability income benefits. The disabled worker must meet an earnings or employment requirement, be disabled as defined in the law, and satisfy a short waiting period. In general, the weekly cash benefits are intended to replace at least half of the wage loss for a limited period, subject to maximum and minimum weekly amounts. The maximum duration of benefits ranges from twenty-six to thirty-nine weeks.

Property and Liability Insurance Programs. A second group of government insurance programs deals with property-liability coverages. Included in this category are such programs as state workers compensation programs, the federal flood insurance program, and some other types of insurance.

Workers Compensation. Workers compensation insurance helps an employer to meet its legal obligations to injured workers under the workers compensation statute of each state. A large proportion of workers compensation insurance is provided by private insurers. However, various states offer workers compensation insurance as an exclusive monopoly insurer or as a competitor, or they provide a residual market.

Six states have monopoly state funds that require all employers to purchase workers compensation insurance from the state fund. Fourteen states have competitive state funds that compete with private insurers.[32]

Some high-risk employers such as loggers and lumber mills may be unable to obtain workers compensation coverage from insurers in the voluntary markets. High-risk employers can obtain coverage from a workers compensation assigned risk pool in which workers compensation insurers are assigned their pro rata share of high risk employers based on premiums written. The National Council on Compensation Insurance manages the assigned risk pool on behalf of thirty-two states through the National Workers Compensation Reinsurance Pool. Incurred losses and collected premiums are determined on an individual state basis and are apportioned to workers compensation insurers based on the proportion of premiums written.

National Flood Insurance. The National Flood Insurance Program is an important government insurance program that indemnifies property owners for flood and mudslide losses. Federal flood insurance is available in all states, the District of Columbia, Puerto Rico, Guam, and the Virgin Islands. Its basic purpose is to make flood insurance *available* to property owners in flood zones at *affordable* rates.

Buildings and most personal property in flood zones are difficult to insure privately because (1) the exposures are not independent, (2) the potential for a catastrophic loss is present, (3) adverse selection is present in that property owners in flood zones are more likely to want flood insurance, and (4) premiums in flood zones would be too high for most insureds to pay without government assistance. The premiums are *affordable* to most persons, which makes the insurance more readily *available* and increase the number of insureds. In addition, the federal government requires the purchase of flood insurance by persons in a participating community who are seeking a mortgage on flood-prone property from a federally insured financial institution. This compulsion increases the number of insureds and reduces adverse selection.

Flood insurance can be purchased from private insurers or directly from the federal government. Under the *write-your-own-program,* private insurers sell the flood insurance under their own names, collect the premiums, retain a specified percentage for commissions and expenses, and pay their own claims. If the insurers' losses are not covered by premiums and investment income, they are reimbursed by the government for the difference. At the end of 1989, 83 percent of the total federal flood insurance policies were written through private insurers under the write-your-own program. The remainder was written directly by the federal government under the National Flood Insurance Program.[33]

Federal Crime Insurance.   Federal crime insurance provides burglary and robbery insurance to individuals and business firms at subsidized rates in certain high crime areas where the Federal Insurance Administration has determined that crime insurance is not available at affordable rates. The primary purpose of the federal crime insurance program is to make crime insurance *available* at *affordable* rates to individuals and firms in high crime areas.

Federal crime insurance is sold by licensed insurance agents and brokers in qualifying jurisdictions. It also is available directly from the servicing organization, National Con-Serv, Inc., a Maryland corporation. The actual insurer is the federal government.

Federal crime insurance has declined in relative importance in recent years. In 1989, it was available in only fourteen states, the District of Columbia, Puerto Rico, and the Virgin Islands, down from twenty-five jurisdictions in 1987. The primary reason for the decline in the number of jurisdictions was the increased availability of burglary and robbery insurance in the private markets. The decline in the number of policies sold can also be explained by relatively low commission rates, lack of enthusiasm by agents and brokers, stringent federal standards for protective devices, and the increased availability of private crime insurance in the standard markets.

Critics argue that the program is no longer needed and should be phased out. Although federal crime insurance has been scheduled to expire several times in the past years, Congress to date has kept the program alive.

Federal Crop Insurance.   Federal crop insurance provides multiple peril coverage for most crops against many unavoidable perils, such as drought, insects, disease, excess rain, and hail. Its purpose is to make crop insurance *available* to farmers at *affordable* rates in order to reduce the financial losses that result from unavoidable crop failures. Crop insurance against certain perils also is available from private insurers.

The insured is guaranteed a certain amount of crop production. If the actual production is less than the guarantee, a loss payment is made for the lost production based on a price selected by the insured before the growing season begins. The program does not guarantee full production, but only a maximum of 75 percent of the average production over a representative period of years. A lower guarantee of 50 percent or 65 percent can be elected with reduced premiums.

The federal crop insurance program has incurred substantial underwriting losses in recent years; participation rates are relatively low because of the widely held view that crop insurance is unnecessary and Congress will provide financial assistance if a drought or natural disaster occurs. The program has been flawed by fraudulent claims, underwriting errors, errors in paying claims, and bureaucratic bungling. At the time of this writing, there is strong congressional support for elimination of the program.

War Risk Insurance. In 1914 Congress established the Bureau of War Risk Insurance that provided insurance on American ships' freight and cargo when insurance was not available elsewhere at reasonable rates. During World War II, the War Shipping Administration provided war risk insurance on U.S. ships and cargo. In addition, in 1942, the Federal War Damage Insurance Corporation was created, which participated with private insurers in providing insurance on property in the United States against damage from enemy attack.[34]

During the 1991 Persian Gulf War, war risk insurance became particularly important when commercial rates for war risk insurance soared. The United States insures at its own expense the merchant ships of any nation that have a contract with the Defense Department to carry military cargo. The United States also offers war risk insurance below commercial rates for merchant ships of any nation that are serving the national defense or economic interests of the United States.[35]

Parcel Post and Registered Mail. Losses in transit to parcel post and registered mail are commercially insurable, but similar protection is available directly from the Postal Service. This competitive approach makes insurance readily available to shippers, as it can be purchased at the post office, together with the postage. Private parcel post and registered mail insurance is an attractive alternative to government insurance for many firms making frequent shipments because it is not necessary to make separate insurance arrangements for each shipment. However, Postal Service insurance is more convenient for shippers who make only a few shipments per year. It also may be less expensive.

Political Risks and Export Credit Insurance. American firms with global operations can purchase political risks and export credit insurance that covers some loss exposures arising out of their global operations. These exposures include war and insurrection, expropriation of property by foreign government, inconvertibility (blockage) of overseas funds, and failure of a foreign purchaser to pay for goods exported from the United States.

More than fifty private insurers participate in the Foreign Credit Insurance Association (FCIA), which works in partnership with the Export-Import Bank of the United States to provide political risk and export credit insurance to United States exporters of goods and services.[36] The Export-Import Bank is an independent federal agency that provides financial support for United States exporters who market their products overseas. Insurance written by the FCIA protects exporters when foreign buyers fail to meet their credit obligations for either commercial or political reasons.[37]

Exposures to loss from expropriation, war, or other political risks are difficult to insure commercially because expected losses are difficult to predict, potential losses can be catastrophic, and the loss exposures may not be independent of one another. However, American firms can insure such exposures by purchasing insurance from the Overseas Private Investment Corporation (OPIC), a government sponsored entity, if the property is located in a less-developed nation and contributes to that nation's economic development. OPIC covers the loss of property that results from expropriation, war, revolution, and currency inconvertibility. The availability of insurance from OPIC encourages American firms to invest in less-developed countries and also promotes the nation's economic interests in a global economy.

Financial Security Programs. A third group of government insurance programs involves situations in which the government guarantees to lenders that their loans, investments, or deposits will be repaid. A primary example is the Federal Deposit Insurance Corporation, which guarantees to depositors the safety of bank deposits.

Federal Deposit Insurance Corporation (FDIC). The Federal Deposit Insurance Corporation (FDIC) insures depositors against loss resulting from the failure or insolvency of banks, state banks, savings banks, and savings and loan institutions. This government insurance reduces potential economic insecurity that could result from the widespread failure of financial institutions.

Private insurance is not considered feasible for banks because commercial banks, savings and loan associations, and other financial institutions are not independent exposures. The same economic conditions that can cause one bank or financial institution to fail may cause other financial institutions to fail at the same time.

National Credit Union Administration (NCUA). The National Credit Union Administration is an independent federal agency that insures the savings and checking accounts of depositors in federal credit unions and in some state chartered credit unions. Federal credit unions are required to have this protection, while state chartered credit unions may elect coverage or, in some cases, may be required to have this protection. Protection for depositors is similar to that provided by the FDIC for depositors in banks and savings and loan associations.

Securities Investor Protection Corporation (SIPC). Some investors in the stock market and other financial markets may experience substantial losses because of the insolvency of brokerage firms that hold securities and cash belonging to their customers. Investors with accounts at brokerage firms are now protected against broker insolvency by the Securities Investor Protection Corporation (SIPC). The SIPC is a federal agency that insures the accounts of customers in brokerage firms up to $500,000 ($100,000 maximum on cash), if the firm should become insolvent. Prior to this form of government insurance, the insolvency of several large brokerage firms resulted in considerable financial loss to investors whose securities and cash were held by those firms.

Pension Benefit Guaranty Corporation (PBGC). The Pension Benefit Guaranty Corporation (PBGC) is a federal corporation that provides plan termination insurance to qualified defined benefit pension plans to protect plan participants from losing their pension benefits if a plan terminates or the employer goes bankrupt.

The PBGC guarantees a certain amount of monthly income to workers who have vested benefits under a qualified defined benefit plan. The PBGC came into existence as a result of the Employee Retirement Income Security Act of 1974 (ERISA). The relatively large number of workers who lost or received reduced pension benefits because of employers' bankruptcy and termination of the pension plan demonstrated the need for government insurance of pensions.

SUMMARY

The primary goals of insurance regulation are to maintain insurer solvency, to protect individual policyholders, and to avoid destructive competition. Insurance regulatory activities are also intended to ensure appropriate and equitable rates, to make insurance available, to make insurance affordable, to enforce insurance laws, and to keep the public informed on insurance matters. These various goals are not always complementary.

Insurers are regulated at the state level by state insurance commissioners. The National Association of Insurance Commissioners serves as a coordinating body among state regulators, thus contributing a degree of uniformity among jurisdictions.

An ongoing controversy revolves around the question of whether insurance should be regulated by the individual states, as provided by the McCarran-Ferguson Act, or by the federal government. Since state regulation is a known quantity but federal regulation is more speculative, many of the arguments are somewhat inconclusive.

The areas actually regulated include the formation and licensing of insurers, the licensing of insurer representatives, solvency regulation, rate regulation, contract regulation, and market conduct. A brief discussion on federal regulation of insurance made it clear that insurance regulation is not confined entirely to state governments.

In addition to regulating private insurers, government bodies themselves offer a wide range of insurance coverages. The role of government insurers can play an exclusive, partnership, or competitive role in relation to private insurers. The reasons for government insurance involve unmet needs, compulsion, convenience, efficiency, and collateral social purposes. The types of insurance that government insurers provide can be broadly characterized as social, property-liability, and financial security.

Chapter Notes

1. See Spencer L. Kimball, "The Regulation of Insurance," in Spencer L. Kimball and Herbert S. Denenberg, eds., *Insurance, Government, and Social Policy* (Homewood, IL: Richard D. Irwin, Inc., 1969), pp. 3-32. The material in this section is based partly on this source. This section also draws on George E. Rejda, *Principles of Risk Management and Insurance*, 4th ed. (New York: Harper Collins Publishers, 1992), Chapter 27.
2. *Issues and Needed Improvements in State Regulation of the Insurance Business (Executive Summary)*, (Washington, D.C.: U.S. General Accounting Office, 1979) p. vii.
3. *Issues and Needed Improvements of the Regulation of the Insurance Business (Executive Summary)*, pp. 11-14.
4. *Issues and Needed Improvements of the Regulation of the Insurance Business (Executive Summary)*, p. 14.
5. Statements of John Washburn in U.S. Congress, House Committee on Energy and Commerce, *Development in State Insurance Regulation*, Hearings Before the Subcommittee on Commerce, Consumer Protection, and Competitiveness (Washington, D.C.: U.S. Government Printing Office, 1988), pp. 8-9.
6. J. D. Hammond, Arnold F. Shapiro, and N. Shilling, *The Regulation of Insurer Solidity Through Capital and Surplus Requirements*, Summary Report NSF Grant APR75-16550 (University Park, Pennsylvania: The Pennsylvania State University, April 1978).
7. This section is based on excerpts from the Insurance Information Institute's Data Base Report, *Captives and Other Risk-Financing Options*, Ruth Gastel, editor, November 1989. Used with permission.
8. NAIC data as cited in the *St. Louis Post-Dispatch*, October 28, 1990, p. 1A.
9. *1991 Property/Casualty Insurance Facts* (New York: Insurance Information Institute, 1991), pp. 12-13.
10. *1990 Life Insurance Fact Book* (Washington, D.C.: American Council of Life Insurance, 1990), p. 103.
11. NAIC data as cited in the *St. Louis Post-Dispatch*, October 28, 1990, p. 1A.
12. General Accounting Office, *Insurance Regulation, The Insurance Regulatory Information System Needs Improvement*, (Washington, D.C.: U.S. Government Printing Office, 1989), p. 8.
13. *1991 Property/Casualty Insurance Facts*, p. 42.
14. *Insurer Failures, Property/Casualty Insurer Insolvencies and State Guaranty Funds*, pp. 26-34.
15. *Insurer Failures, Property/Casualty Insurer Insolvencies and State Guaranty Funds*, (Oldwick, N.J.: A. M. Best Company, 1991), p. 28.
16. U.S. Congress, House, Committee on Energy and Commerce, *Failed Promises, Insurance Company Insolvencies, A Report by the Subcommittee on Oversight and Investigations* (Washington, D.C.: U.S. Government Printing Office, 1990), p. 2.

17. *Failed Promises, Insurance Company Insolvencies,* pp. 1-76. See also, U.S. Congress, house, Committee on Energy and Commerce, *Insurance Company Failures,* Hearings Before the Subcommittee on Oversight and Investigations (Washington, D.C.: U.S. Government Printing Office, 1988).
18. *Failed Promises, Insurance Company Insolvencies,* p. 10.
19. General Accounting Office, *Insurance Regulation, Problems in the State Monitoring of Property/Casualty Insurer Solvency,* (Washington, D.C.: U.S. Government Printing Office, 1989), pp. 2-26.
20. *Insurance Regulation, Problems in the State Monitoring of Property/ Casualty Insurer Solvency,* p. 20.
21. *Insurance Regulation, Problems in the State Monitoring of Property/ Casualty Insurer Solvency,* p. 4.
22. Bernard L. Webb, J. J. Launie, Willis Park Rokes, and Norman A. Baglini, *Insurance Company Operations,* 3rd ed., vol. II (Malvern, PA: American Institute for Property and Liability Underwriters, 1984), p. 7.
23. Scott E. Harrington, "Competition and Regulation in the Automobile Insurance Market" (paper prepared for distribution at the ABA National Institute on Insurance Competition and Pricing in the 1990s, Baltimore, Maryland, June 2-3, 1990), p. 6.
24. The empirical studies cited in this section are based on Henry Grabowski, W. Kip Viscusi, and William N. Evans, "Price and Availability Tradeoffs of Automobile Insurance Regulation," *The Journal of Risk and Insurance,* vol. 56, no. 2, June 1989, pp. 277-279. An exhaustive analysis of the various studies of the impact of rate regulation on prices and underwriting results in property and liability insurance can be found in Scott Harrington, "The Impact of Rate Regulation on Prices and Underwriting Results in the Property-Liability Insurance Industry: A Survey," *The Journal of Risk and Insurance,* vol. 51, no. 4, December 1984, pp. 577-623. See also, Scott E. Harrington, "The Relationship Between Voluntary and Involuntary Market Rates and Rate Regulation in Automobile Insurance," *The Journal of Risk and Insurance,* vol. 57, no. 1, March 1990, pp. 9-27.
25. *1991 Property/Casualty Insurance Facts,* p. 10.
26. This section on contract regulation is based partly on two articles by Spencer L. Kimball and Werner Pfennigstorf. The first is "Legislative and Judicial Control of the Terms of Insurance Contracts: A Comparative Study of American and European Practice," *Indiana Law Journal,* vol. 39, no. 4, Summer 1964, pp. 675-731. The second is "Administrative Control of the Terms of Insurance Contracts: A Comparative Study," *Indiana Law Journal,* vol. 40, no. 2, Winter 1965, pp. 143-231.
27. *Issues and Needed Improvements in State Regulation of the Insurance Business (Executive Summary),* pp. 16-17.
28. S.E.C. v. Variable Annuity Life Insurance Co. of America et al., 359 U.S. 65 (1959).
29. Adapted from Mark R. Greene, "Government Insurers," *Issues in Insurance,* 4th ed., vol. I (Malvern, PA: American Institute for Property and Liability Underwriters, 1987), pp. 195-199.
30. Domenico Gagliardo, *American Social Insurance* rev. ed. (New York: Harper Bros., 1955), pp. 14-21.

31. Reinhardt A. Hohaus, "Equity, Adequacy and Related Factors in Old Age Security," in William Haber and Wilbur J. Cohen, eds., *Social Security* (Homewood, IL: Richard D. Irwin, Inc., 1960), pp. 61-62.
32. Monopoly workers compensation funds are in Nevada, North Dakota, Ohio, Washington, West Virginia, and Wyoming. Competitive workers compensation funds are in Arizona, California, Colorado, Idaho, Maryland, Michigan, Minnesota, Montana, New York, Oklahoma, Oregon, Pennsylvania, Rhode Island, and Utah.
33. *1991 Property/Casualty Insurance Facts*, pp. 46-48.
34. Emmett J. Vaughan, *Fundamentals of Risk and Insurance*, 5th ed. (New York: John Wiley & Sons, 1989), pp. 133-134.
35. Steven Prokesch, "Insuring 'War Risks' at Lloyd's," *The New York Times*, January 16, 1991.
36. *Sharing the Risk, How the Nation's Business, Homes and Autos Are Insured*, 3rd ed. (New York: Insurance Information Institute, 1989), pp. 145-146.
37. *Sharing the Risk*, p. 124.

Bibliography

Asher, Robert. "Failure and Fulfillment: Agitation for Employers' Liability Legislation and the Origins of Workmen's Compensation in New York State, 1876-1910." *Labor History,* Spring 1983, pp. 198-222.

Bickelhaupt, David Lynn. *Transition to Multiple-Line Insurance Companies.* Homewood, IL: Richard D. Irwin, Inc., 1961.

Carr, William H.A. *Perils: Named and Unnamed.* New York, NY: McGraw-Hill Book Company, 1967.

Clough, Shepard B. *A Century of American Life Insurance.* New York, NY: Columbia University Press, 1946.

Cohen, I. Bernard. *Benjamin Franklin: His Contribution to the American Tradition.* New York, NY: The Bobbs-Merrill Company, 1953.

Daniel, Hawthorne. *The Hartford of Hartford.* New York, NY: Random House, 1960.

de Roover, Florence Elder, "Early Examples of Marine Insurance." *Journal of Economic History,* vol. 5, November 1945, p. 197.

Development in State Insurance Regulation, Hearings Before the Subcommittee on Commerce, Consumer Protection, and Competitiveness. Washington, DC: U.S. Government Printing Office, 1988.

Doerflinger, Thomas M. *A Vigorous Spirit of Enterprise: Merchants and Economic Development in Revolutionary Philadelphia.* Chapel Hill, NC: University of North Carolina Press, 1986.

"An Early Fire Insurance Company." *South Carolina Historical and Genealogical Magazine,* January 1907, pp. 46-53.

Fitzpatrick, Clarke J. and Buse, Elliott. *Fifty Years of Suretyship and Insurance.* Baltimore, MD, 1946.

Gagliardo, Domenico. *American Social Insurance.* Rev. ed. New York, NY: Harper Bros., 1955.

Gastel, Ruth, ed. *Captives and Other Risk-Financing Options.* New York, NY: Insurance Information Institute, 1989.

General Accounting Office. *Insurance Regulation, The Insurance Regulatory Information System Needs Improvement.* Washington, DC: U.S. Government Printing Office, 1990.

____. *Insurance Regulation, Problems in the State Monitoring of Property / Casualty Insurer Solvency.* Washington, DC: U.S. Government Printing Office, 1989.

Grabowski, Henry; Viscusi, W. Kip; and Evans, William N. "Price and Availability Tradeoffs of Automobile Insurance Regulation." *The Journal of Risk and Insurance,* vol. 56, no. 2, June 1989, pp. 277-279.

Grant, H. Roger. *Insurance Reform: Consumer Action in the Progressive Era.* Ames, IA: The Iowa State University Press, 1979.

Greene, Mark R. "Government Insurers." *Issues in Insurance,* 4th ed., vol. I. Malvern, PA: American Institute for Property and Liability Underwriters, 1987.

Hammond, J.D.; Shapiro, Arnold F.; and Shilling, N. *The Regulation of Insurer Solidity Through Capital and Surplus Requirements.* University Park, PA: The Pennsylvania State University, 1978.

Harrington, Scott E. "Competition and Regulation in the Automobile Insurance Market." Paper prepared for distribution at the ABA National Institute on Insurance Competition and Pricing in the 1990s, Baltimore, MD, 1990.

____. "The Impact of Rate Regulation on Prices and Underwriting Results in the Property-Liability Insurance Industry: A Survey." *The Journal of Risk and Insurance,* vol. 51, no. 4, December 1984, pp. 577-623.

____. "The Relationship Between Voluntary Market Rates and Rate Regulation in Automobile Insurance." *The Journal of Risk and Insurance,* vol. 57, no. 1, March 1990, pp. 9-27.

Head, Alice Ann and Head, George L. "On Risk Management: The Power of Politics in Safety." *National Underwriter* (Property and Casualty), July 22, 1991, p. 17.

Hohaus, Reinhardt A. "Equity, Adequacy and Related Factors in Old Age Security," in William Haber and Wilbur J. Cohen, eds. *Social Security.* Homewood, IL: Richard D. Irwin, Inc., 1960.

Hovenkamp, Herbert. *Enterprise and the American Law.* Cambridge, MA: Harvard University Press, 1991.

Hughes, David. *A Treatise on the Law Related to Insurance in These Parts.* O. Halstead, Collins and Hannay, and Gould and Banks; Grigg and Elliott, 1833.

Insurance Company Failures. Hearings Before the Subcommittee on Oversight and Investigations. Washington, DC: U.S. Government Printing Office, 1988.

Insurer Failures, Property / Casualty Insurer Solvencies and State Guaranty Funds, Oldwick, NJ: A.M. Best Company, 1991.

Israel, Jonathan I. *Dutch Primacy in World Trade, 1585-1740.* Oxford: Oxford University Press, 1989.

Issues and Needed Improvements in State Regulation of the Insurance Business (Executive Summary). Washington, DC: U.S. General Accounting Office, 1979.

James, Marquis. *Biography of a Business: Insurance Company of North America, 1792-1943.* Indianapolis, IN: The Bobbs-Merrill Company, 1942.

Keller, Morton. *The Life Insurance Enterprise, 1885-1910.* Cambridge, MA: Harvard University Press, 1963.

____. *Regulating a New Economy.* Cambridge, MA: Harvard University Press, 1990.

Kimball, Spencer L. "The Regulation of Insurance," in Spencer L. Kimball and Herbert S. Denenberg, *Insurance, Government, and Social Policy.* Homewood, IL: Richard D. Irwin, Inc., 1969.

Kimball, Spencer L. and Pfenigstorf, Werner. "Administrative Control of the Terms of Insurance Contracts: A Comparative Study." *Indiana Law Journal,* vol. 40, no. 2, Winter 1965, pp. 143-231.

____. "Legislative and Judicial Control of the Terms of Insurance Contracts: A Comparative Study of American and European Practice." *Indiana Law Journal,* vol. 39, no. 4, Summer 1964, pp. 675-731.

Krooss, Herman E. "Financial Institutions." *The Growth of the Seaport Cities, 1790-1825,* David T. Gilchrist, ed. Charlottesville, VA: The University Press of Virginia, 1976.

McClosky, Donald. *Prosperous Peasants.* Princeton, NJ: Princeton University Press, 1992.

Michelbacher, G.F. *Multiple Line Insurance.* New York, NY: McGraw-Hill Book Company, 1957.

National Association of Insurance Commissioners, All-Industry Rating Bills, June 12, 1946.

The New York Board of Fire Underwriters, 1867-1967. New York, NY: New York Board of Fire Underwriters, 1967.

1990 Life Insurance Fact Book. Washington, DC: American Council of Life Insurance, 1990.

1991 Property/Casualty Insurance Facts. New York, NY: Insurance Information Institute, 1991.

Nye, Russell B. *Midwestern Progressive Politics.* New York, NY: Harper & Row, 1965.

The Papers of Benjamin Franklin. Vol. 2. The Pennsylvania Gazette, February 4, 1734.

The Papers of Benjamin Franklin. Vol. 3. New Haven: Yale University Press, 1960-1974.

Pearson, Robin. "Thrift or Dissipation? The Business of Life Assurance in the Early Nineteenth Century." The Economic History Review, vol. XLIII, May 1990, pp. 236-254.

Perry, James F. "The McCarran-Ferguson Act: An Invitation to State Action." *CPCU Journal,* vol. 44, September 1991, pp. 162-173.

Pfeffer, Irving. "The Early History of Insurance." *The Annals,* vol. 19, Summer 1966, pp. 101-112.

Proceedings of the National Convention of Insurance Commissioners, 1914.

Prokesch, Steven. "Insuring the 'War Risks' at Lloyd's." *The New York Times,* January 16, 1991.

Rapone, Anita. *The Guardian Life Insurance Company, 1860-1920.* New York, NY: New York University Press, 1963.

Rejda, George E. *Principles of Risk Management and Insurance.* 4th ed. New York, NY: Harper Collins Publishers, 1992.

Report on the Joint Committee of the Senate and Assembly of the State of New York Appointed to Investigate Corrupt Practices in Connection with Legislation, and the Affairs of Insurance Companies Other Than Those Doing Life Insurance Business. Albany, NY, 1911.

St. Louis Post-Dispatch, October 28, 1990, p. 1A.

Sharing the Risk, How the Nation's Business, Homes and Autos Are Insured. 3rd ed. New York, NY: Insurance Information Institute, 1989.

Slaski, Eugene R. "Thomas Willing: Moderation during the American Revolution." Ph.D. diss., Florida State University, 1971

Spooner, Frank C. *Risks at Sea: Amsterdam Insurance and Maritime Europe, 1766-1780.* Cambridge: Cambridge University Press, 1983.

Stalson, J. Owen. *Marketing Life Insurance: History in America.* Homewood, IL: Richard D. Irwin, Inc., 1969.

Stigler, Stephen M. *The History of Statistics: The Measurement of Uncertainty Before 1900.* Cambridge, MA: Harvard University Press, 1986.

Tracy, James D. *A Financial Revolution in the Hapsburg Netherlands.* Berkeley, CA: University of California Press, 1985.

The Travelers 100 Years. Hartford, CT: The Travelers, 1964.

U.S. Congress, House, Committee on Energy and Commerce. *Failed Promises, Insurance Company Insolvencies, A Report by the Subcommittee on Oversight and Investigations.* Washington, DC: U.S. Government Printing Office, 1990.

van der Wee, Hermann. "Money, Credit, and Banking Systems." *The Cambridge Economic History of Europe,* vol. V, pp. 337-338.

Vaughan, Emmett J. *Fundamentals of Risk and Insurance.* 5th ed. New York, NY: John Wiley & Sons, 1989.

Weaver, Glenn. *The Hartford Steam Boiler Inspection and Insurance Company.* Hartford, CT, 1966.

Webb, Bernard L. "Notes on the Early History of American Insurance." *CPCU Annals,* vol. 29, June 1976, pp. 92-93.

Webb, Bernard L.; Launie, J.J.; Rokes, Willis Park; and Baglini, Norman A. *Insurance Company Operations.* 3rd ed., vol. II. Malvern, PA: American Institute for Property and Liability Underwriters, 1984.

Weller, Charles D. "The McCarran-Ferguson Act's Antitrust Exemption for Insurance: Language, History and Policy." *Duke Law Journal,* 1978, pp. 587-643.

Wenck, Thomas L. "The Historical Development of Standard Policies." *The Journal of Risk and Insurance,* December 1968, pp. 537-550.

Winter, William D. "The Need for Research." Address to The Mariners Club in Philadelphia, May 3, 1954, in *The Multiple Line Concept and the Need for Research*. New York, NY: Atlantic Mutual Insurance Company, 1954.

Zelizer, Viviana A. Rotman. *Morals and Markets: The Development of Life Insurance in the United States*. New York, NY: Columbia University Press, 1979.

Index